FLIGHT SIMULATOR
CO-PILOT

CHARLES GULICK

FLIGHT SIMULATOR
CO-PILOT

MICROSOFT
PRESS

THE FLIGHT SIMULATOR CO-PILOT Series

PUBLISHED BY
Microsoft Press
A Division of Microsoft Corporation
16011 N. E. 36th Way, Box 97017, Redmond, Washington 98073-9717

Library of Congress Cataloging in Publication Data
Gulick, Charles.
Flight simulator co-pilot.
1. Flight Simulators.   2. Airplanes—Piloting—Data processing.
I. Title.
TL 712.5G85   1986   269.132'52'078   86-21784
ISBN 1-55615-001-6

Printed and bound in the United States of America.

1 2 3 4 5 6 7 8 9 FGFG 8 9 0 9 8 7 6

Distributed to the book trade in the United States by Harper & Row.

Distributed to the book trade in Canada by General Publishing Company, Ltd.

Distributed to the book trade outside the United States and Canada
by Penguin Books Ltd.

Penguin Books Ltd., Harmondsworth, Middlesex, England
Penguin Books Australia Ltd., Ringwood, Victoria, Australia
Penguin Books N. Z. Ltd., 182-190 Wairau Road, Auckland 10, New Zealand

British Cataloging in Publication Data available

Contents

I. BASIC FLIGHT INSTRUCTION

    While the instructor flies the plane, get aquainted with the instrument panel
and the aircraft's control surfaces.

    Learn to recognize the primary flight configuration of straight and level
solely by referencing your cockpit instruments.

    Climb and descend at specific rates under precise control, with airspeed
constant, and with or without outside visual reference.

    Witness a 20-degree turn, followed by entering and rolling out of 25-, 30-, and
35-degree turns.

    Use your instrument panel and out-the-windshield references to make con-
trolled turns while climbing.

    Understand the techniques specific to your aircraft for maintaining a given
altitude within 20 feet.

    Learn when, why, and how to make the transition from slowflight to normal
flight and back again.

    Learn how runways are numbered and review an actual preflight inspection.
Then execute a precision takeoff and climb-out.

    See what a correct landing should look like while you control the aircraft
from a preset approach configuration.

Preface

This book goes beyond my previous two, in describing specific techniques for flying the Cessna (Microsoft) and Piper (SubLogic) flight simulators created by program designer Bruce Artwick and his team at SubLogic Corporation. Many readers of *40 Great...* and *40 More Great Flight Simulator Adventures* will find here a more comprehensive, wider ranging, and more explicit methodology, and a few instructions that are slightly at odds with those in the earlier books. These differences reflect my own experience over many hundreds of hours of flying these aircraft, during which I have worked to refine the techniques described, searching always for more consistent and precise control and more realistic inflight performance.

In simulator flying, as in any endeavor we undertake—from sailing a boat to skiing to writing a poem to playing chess—excellence is the driver, the motivating force. There is genuine satisfaction in flying these computer-screen airplanes well, and the more we fly them the more believable we find them to be. The flight simulators have erroneously been called "games." They are not games. They are what they say they are: simulations. And to my mind, they are the most advanced simulations offered to microcomputerists today. They challenge us from the moment we start them up until the moment we shut them down. Enhanced by our ability to imagine, their monotonous stretches of green and blue become the green of real earth and the blue of true sky. The wings that bear us aloft have actual lift, and the runways are as alluring and challenging as they are in the real world.

If we set time to a minute or so after dawn in the Editor, then exit to fly, it becomes early morning out there even though the scene is no different from noon. All we have to do is fantasize a little, and we can smell the morning freshness. We can see the dew on that too-green grass. We can sense that the sun is somewhat new, even in that absolute and all-too-flawless blue.

In simulator flight, as in actual flight, there can be moments that are hypnotic in their sense of suspension, somehow, in another dimension, not quite related to time nor quite a part of space. They are moments, in the truest sense, apart. Real and unreal change places, and we are transported. There are some scenes at dusk, in the simulated Seattle for instance, that I wouldn't trade for genuine earth, by genuine water, under an actual evening sky. I have seen jewels on the ground down there, pinpoints of spurious gold specks which, placed just where they are and when they are, have a beauty and reality all their own. Too, the very sparseness of the simulation sometimes forces us to concentrate on essentials of a sort that we miss in reality, like a photograph mostly unfocused, or some of the silences in music.

I've been flying the simulator ever since it was there to fly, and I confess that I still approach an airport I've never seen before with intense excitement and elation. Usually, I know, it will look like fifty others. But sometimes, it won't. If it's near a city or a body of water or a mountain, it may be a thing of the rarest beauty, just the way it lies there on the rest of the geography, and just because I'm approaching it from this specific direction out of hundreds I might have selected, or by sheerest chance.

So come, let's fly together, and get good at it and believe together in the believability of what we're doing. I'll teach you all I know, and perhaps — doing that — show you some of what I see.

Charles Gulick
Lake Park, Florida
August, 1986

Introduction

*F**light Simulator Co-Pilot* is a companion book to the Microsoft Flight Simulator, for IBM PC, PCjr, and compatible computers, and the SubLogic FSII Flight Simulator, for Commodore 64, Apple II series, and Atari 800, XL and XE computers. Some flights call for the SubLogic Scenery Disks (Western set: Disks 2, 3, 4, and 5) and serve as an introduction to that remarkable new and dramatic Flight Simulator concept.

Co-Pilot is not reading matter to be absorbed while the computer is turned off, but to be experienced while you fly the modes it describes, using the parameters that are provided at the beginning of each chapter. That way you will follow and perform a wide variety of operations, from simple to advanced, and cover hundreds of miles of simulator geography while you learn and enjoy. In short, this is a book to be flown rather than simply read.

You are introduced to simulator flying as you would be to actual flying, beginning with a familiarization flight much like you would encounter if you went to an airport to learn how to fly. This is followed by in-the-air demonstrations and explanations of specific attitudes and maneuvers basic to precision aircraft control. You'll learn what "straight and level" is, how to perform precision climbs, descents, standard and steep turns, how to hold a desired altitude, how to make transitions into and out of slowflight, and how to fly airport patterns.

Before you make your first controlled takeoff and climb-out, you'll have acquired procedural understanding well beyond that of the average simulator pilot, and of many actual student pilots. Even if you're an accomplished pilot already, you are urged to go along with the method of instruction presented, which is specific to the simulators, and compare the results with the way you're flying now.

In *Co-Pilot*, nothing is left to chance and nothing is done haphazardly. If you have the will to understand and patience to practice the techniques described, particularly those in Section I, you *will* fly Flight Simulator with increasing precision, and with a solid knowledge of what you're doing and why.

In Section II, after your basic flight training, you're introduced to the techniques of aircraft navigation and instrument flying. By the time you make your first flight through an overcast, and your first night flight, you'll have a large measure of confidence. And soon you'll be into aerobatics and special maneuvers like aileron rolls, the chandelle, and Eights Along a Road. And you'll be ready to undertake advanced operations such as an ILS (Instrument Landing System) approach. But no matter how proficient you become, you will never stop learning. No pilot ever does.

As the book progresses into Section III, you'll discover how the skills you acquired early in your training pay off. You'll take real and deserved pride in the professional way you handle your airplane. You'll be able to "talk flying" intelligently with any pilot, from simulator novices to airline captains. And don't be surprised if you find them listening, intently.

Pilot Advisories

Entering Editor Parameters

Since virtually every chapter requires you to set up a new and different flight situation, ability to use the Editor is mandatory. Consult your manual if you are not familiar with the techniques for changing the Editor parameters.

Press the Editor key

Simulation Control parameters — sound, auto-coordination, etc. — are omitted from the listings at the head of each chapter in the interest of brevity, and because you will set most of them to suit yourself. Just remember that 0 means off or disabled, and 1 means on or enabled. To slow down the communication rate (rate at which Air Traffic Information Service (ATIS) messages scroll across your screen) use a lower number, and to speed it up, a higher number. Use powers of 2 for smoothest results, 128 being a good middle value. (See "About Reality Mode" on page xv).

Shear altitudes are also omitted from the parameter listings, but are assumed to be set — in descending order — to 9000, 6000, and 3000 feet. These are the defaults on some simulator versions. If they are not the defaults on your version, enter those values when you first go into the Editor. They'll remain in effect, though they may vary slightly, until you turn off the computer.

Clouds will always be indicated in the parameter listings. If no clouds are to be encountered, a 0 will appear; otherwise, clouds will be listed in the order of layer, tops, bottoms — in the form Cloud Layer 1: 9000, 7000. Winds aloft are listed only if they are present. Surface wind is always listed.

Information You Need While Flying

Though the various versions of Flight Simulator perform similarly, there are numerous differences in command and control keys. Therefore, I have tried to avoid references to the keyboard in favor of general terms. Your preparation for flying the book thus consists of familiarity with the keys that control aileron, elevator, throttle, flaps, NAV and COM radios, and out-the-windshield and radar views. The Appendix in the back of this book provides a ready reference to these keys.

Press the Save key

Press the Recall key

Press the Pause key

Saving Modes

It's important to save the parameters for each chapter as you set them up and before you exit the Editor. Then you can use the Recall key to return to the beginning of a flight should you wish to for any reason. This will often be necessary to put the airplane on the prescribed heading, since the simulator frequently points you incorrectly when you exit the Editor. A crash, for example, would return you to the current flight if you saved the mode, but to Meigs Field or the bottom of Lake Michigan if you didn't.

You may wish to save some or all modes permanently to disk. Instructions for this are thoroughly covered in the individual simulator manuals.

Using Pause to Catch Up

Remember that you can always use the Pause key, on the ground or in flight, to consult your references or to read ahead a few sentences in a chapter so you will be prepared for what is to come. At critical points, pauses are suggested in the text.

About the Colors

Co-Pilot was created while simultaneously flying the Microsoft and SubLogic versions, on an IBM PC compatible and Commodore 64, respectively. The colors described are those obtained with a composite monitor, which affords the greatest realism. If you are flying with a monochrome monitor, I urge you to switch to a color display of some kind, even a TV set, to avoid missing much of the beauty and appeal of the program.

Special Situations

APPLE: The "operational neutral" elevator parameter described in the book may not be correct for the Apple version. If you are using an Apple and experience any discrepancies (they should show up in the "Basic Flight Instruction" section), change the Piper value given from 36863 to 34815. The difference (2048) between these values may also be applied to other flight situations if needed. For example, if the elevator parameter given for Piper in the "Slowflight/Normal Cruise Transition" chapter, 40959, does not produce the desired result, reduce it by 2048, entering a value of 38911. If this isn't satisfactory, arrive at the correct figure empirically by adjusting the elevator to achieve the flight condition described, then enter the Editor briefly to find and make a note of the value.

ATARI: The Atari version will, for most flights described, require you to insert the Scenery Disk provided with the program. This is not to be confused with the SubLogic Scenery Disks, separate software products that are, or are scheduled to be, available for all of the computers. Numerous chapters call for use of certain western U.S. area Scenery Disks.

CESSNA: Because only the Cessna, or Microsoft, version has retractable landing gear, the book assumes all flights will be with the gear in the down position, as if fixed. Planes flown by students and beginning pilots usually have fixed gear anyway, so this should not be cause for distress. If it is, the Cessna pilot is welcome to retract the gear, but the increased speed will affect some of the flight description.

Cessna vs. Piper

Because of differences in the simulator programs, certain instrument readings and parameter settings in the Editor vary depending on whether you are flying Cessna or Piper.

Why No ADF

Since the Cessna version does not have Automatic Direction Finding equipment, use of the ADF is not covered in the book.

Always Check Heading First

Before you exit the Editor to begin a flight, save the mode and check the Heading parameter. Then when you've exited, if the heading indicator on your instrument panel does not read within a degree or two of the correct parameter (very often the case), press the Recall key. This should result in the correct heading within a degree.

About Reality Mode

I have chosen to exclude the Reality mode from the flights in this book due to what I feel are its deficiencies with respect to elevator trim. With Reality disabled—set to 0 in the Editor—the elevator is more sensitive and allows finer adjustments than does the Reality mode trim control. At the same time, it realistically simulates trim control because it stays where you put it, as does the trim control in the prototype or actual Cessna and Piper aircraft. The elevator returns to its neutral position when any backward or (much less often) forward pressure applied on the control yoke is relaxed, much as the steering wheel in a car finds its center position if let go. Because we cannot actually feel control pressures in the simulator, the interaction of trim and elevator setting in Reality mode, changing the elevator position automatically, is simply unrealistic. This is too bad, because other aspects of Reality do provide more realism overall. But the compromise has been made in favor of more precise pilot control in actual flight. (If you wish to fly Reality mode, it should pose no major problems. You'll just need to compensate a bit.)

Reliability

Reliability, effective in Reality mode only, is assumed to be set to 100 throughout this book. But if you're flying with Reality enabled and feel like flying a mode with a lower reliability setting just for the challenge, go ahead.

Last Word

The instructional information in this book relates solely to simulator flying. While most of the concepts presented are authentic with respect to actual flying technique, only side-by-side instruction for many hours, with an FAA-qualified flight instructor, can prepare you for flight in the actual aircraft.

Also, any and all references to and comparisons of Cessna and Piper in this book apply solely to the so-named simulated aircraft and not, of course, to the actual Cessna and Piper aircraft. All differences mentioned derive from differences in computer sophistication and processing speeds, not to inherent differences in design or performance of the aircraft.

Now climb in the left seat, start your engine, and let's fly!

BASIC

Flight Instruction

Flight and Panel Familiarization

Eagle Field Training Base (Local)

North: 17415. East: 7446. Altitude: 410. Pitch: 0. Bank: 0. Heading: Cessna 330. Heading: Piper 331. Airspeed: 0. Throttle: 32767. Rudder: 32767. Ailerons: 32767. Flaps: 0. Elevators: Cessna 37119. Elevators: Piper 40959. Time: 7:00. Season: 2. Clouds: 0. Surface Wind: 3 kn., 330 deg.

Airspeed indicator

Attitude indicator

Altimeter

Vertical-speed indicator

We're in the process of a takeoff from Runway 33, Eagle Field (the simulator's World War I base). For most of this flight, I'll handle the airplane. Use your eyes and follow along with what I'm explaining. If you want to point at the instruments on your panel as I describe them, it may help fix their location in your mind.

First, pay attention to the airspeed indicator, the round instrument at the top left of your instrument panel. The needle indicates our airspeed in knots. On a takeoff run, like this, it tells us when we have flying speed. Notice that we're gaining speed as we roll.

Watch out front now until we leave the runway.

To the right of the airspeed indicator is the artificial horizon, also called the attitude indicator. The horizon and the earth are depicted on the lower half, and the sky on the upper half of the display. The two longer lines and the dot at the center represent, respectively, the wings and the nose of the aircraft. Right now the attitude indicator shows the nose slightly high in relation to the horizon, which in our present configuration means we're about to take off. After we take off, it's one indication that we're climbing.

To the right of the artificial horizon is the altimeter, an instrument which tells us our altitude above sea level in hundreds and also thousands of feet. When the longer needle is moving clockwise, as now, it confirms that we're climbing.

Directly under the altimeter is the vertical-speed indicator, or VSI, which tells us our rate of climb. The numbers on the top half of the dial mark off climb rates of 500, 1000, and 1500 feet per minute. You simply add two zeroes to the reading. The same numbers on the bottom half mark off descent rates. The needle tells us whether we're climbing or descending, and by how many feet per minute.

Look out the windshield now, and take in everything, from one side to the other. Let it register in your mind. Notice the mountain you're flying toward, the ground and marker lines, and the river, if you can still see them. Don't look absentmindedly. Really observe. This is part of flying intelligently and well; as an instructor might say, "Keep your head on a swivel."

After a few passes across the windshield, drop your eyes to the airspeed indicator (top left on your panel—remember?) and begin a scan of all six of the instruments on the left side of your panel, working clockwise. We've already examined four of them: airspeed indicator, artificial horizon, altimeter, and vertical-speed indicator. To the left of the VSI is the heading indicator, which tells us toward what point of the compass we are flying, based on the 360-degree circle. 360 degrees, or 0, is north, 90 degrees is east, 180 degrees is south, and 270 degrees is west. So we're aiming 30 degrees to the west of due north. The next instrument, at the bottom left of your panel, is the turn coordinator. It tells us whether the wings are level, as they are now, or whether we're banking, and, if so, how steeply and in which direction. You'll learn more about banking a little later in this training. I don't expect you to absorb everything the first time out.

Heading indicator

Turn coordinator

As you scan these six primary instruments and the world beyond your windshield, let the values and the sense of what you're seeing, both inside and outside the airplane, sink in. Out the window, what do you see and what don't you see anymore? On the panel, what are the instruments telling you? The airspeed indicator is steady at about 80 in Cessna, 85 in Piper. The artificial horizon is showing considerably more sky than earth now. The altimeter needle is moving clockwise, confirming that we're climbing to an ever-higher altitude. The VSI is indicating our rate of climb—presently better than 1000 FPM (feet per minute). The heading indicator is staying put at around 330 to 332, because we haven't turned from our original course. The little wings on the turn indicator are level, confirming that we're not in a bank to either left or right; the wings are level.

Of course I know about the mountain. I certainly wouldn't have you crash into a mountain on your first flight. Watch, and you'll see we fly right over it.

If you have saved the mode, press the Recall key to repeat takeoff at this point if desired.

I hope you're relaxed now. Take plenty of time to read what follows; do as I ask, and practice your scanning while we fly.

One of the biggest problems beginning pilots face is the tendency to overcontrol; they use too much control for too long, trying to get a desired result. With your help, I'll demonstrate this:

If you are flying Cessna, press your down-elevator key three times in quick succession.

Press the Save key

Press the Recall key

If you are flying Piper, press your down-elevator key twice in quick succession, wait a second, then press the up-elevator key once.

Fix your eyes (for this demonstration only; we don't usually "fix" our eyes on anything when flying) on the VSI (the rate-of-climb indicator).

Even though you're still under full power, the needle swings violently downward. Where a few seconds ago you were climbing at better than 1000 FPM, suddenly you're descending at nearly the same rate. Then, just as suddenly, you're climbing again, at well above 1000 FPM, until finally the airplane settles into a climb of 800 to 900 FPM in Cessna, and about 500 FPM in Piper.

What happened?

In effect, you applied abrupt forward pressure to the control wheel (henceforth we'll call it "the yoke"), by moving the elevators rapidly from a high "up" setting to a neutral position. And that one act radically upset the balance of forces that were controlling the climb. The plane, suddenly told to stop nosing up altogether, quickly nosed down. The propeller, instead of screwing through the air in an upward direction (the British, with good reason, call the propeller an "airscrew"), began screwing downward. This and the weight of the plane caused a buildup of airspeed, which increased the relative wind—the air moving past the wings. The airfoil (shape of the wings) converted the relative wind to lift (an upward-pushing force on the wings), causing the airplane to pass back through level flight and then resume climbing. As the speed added by the descent bled off, the plane gradually lowered its nose again and assumed the climb natural to it in its present environment. (By "present environment" I mean this particular altitude, the current air density, your neutral elevator setting, and your engine at full power.)

Sometime hold a piece of paper at the edge, and angle it downward a bit while moving it a short distance rapidly through the air. You'll see the front edge rise. That's a rough demonstration of lift. The wind against the sheet of paper, created by your thrusting it forward, represents relative wind.

Changing RPM

We've been at full power now longer than is reasonable. So let's make a power reduction.

RPM indicator

At or near the bottom right of your instrument panel is the RPM indicator. Using your throttle-control keys, reduce your power setting for an RPM reading of 2205 in Cessna, and 2200 in Piper.

After this power reduction, do your regular instrument scan. Your airspeed won't vary much. The attitude indicator will soon show your wings and nose on a level with the artificial horizon. The altimeter will gradually steady at about 6800 feet in Cessna, and 6000 feet in Piper. The VSI will oscillate a

bit, until your aircraft finds its natural altitude for this power setting; then the
needle will sit motionless at the 9 o'clock, or center, position. (In my Cessna,
the VSI needle is pretty accurate. In my Piper, the needle sits a little high. But
in either case, we have other ways of knowing if we're climbing—for instance
the altimeter and artificial horizon.)

Our heading remains unchanged, because we've entered no banks and
made no turns. The turn coordinator shows the wings level.

Additional Panel Familiarization

Now let's continue familiarizing ourselves with the instrument panel.
Look at the six primary instruments again (shown in Figure 1-1). Read them
left to right, starting at the upper left, clockwise:

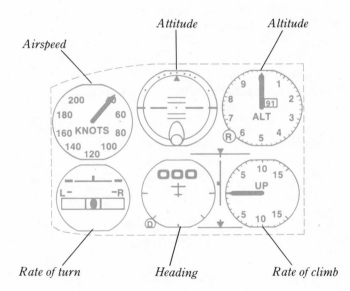

Figure 1-1. The six primary instruments

The instrument between airspeed and altitude is called the "artificial
horizon," because that's exactly what it is. If you were flying in an overcast
and couldn't see the ground, you would believe what this instrument told you
about the attitude of the airplane in relation to earth, horizon, and sky (which
is why it's also called an "attitude indicator"). Right now it tells you that we're
straight and level, which the rate of climb confirms.

5

The altimeter shows us steady at 6800 in Cessna, and 6000 in Piper. The rate-of-climb needle sits at zero. The heading indicator stays on 330 to 332, and the turn indicator shows no bank, no turn.

Now for a look at the rest of the instrument panel. I suggest that you read a sentence or two, then look up and examine each instrument.

Ailerons, Elevators, and Rudder

In an "I" arrangement between the VSI and the heading indicator are three important indicators. From the top down, they show aileron-control position, elevator-control position, and rudder-control position. In our flights, unless you elect to enable Reality mode, the aileron and rudder are coordinated, and their indicators will move together.

The ailerons are hinged, movable surfaces on the trailing edge of the wings, which enable us to bank and turn the aircraft (see Figure 1-2). If we apply left aileron, for example, the aileron on the left wing goes up and the aileron on the right wing goes down. This gives the left wing less lift and gives the right wing more lift, causing the airplane to bank and roll to the left—in the direction of the low wing. The aileron-position indicator shows how much aileron we're applying in the direction of turn.

Aileron-position indicator

Elevator-position indicator

Rudder-position indicator

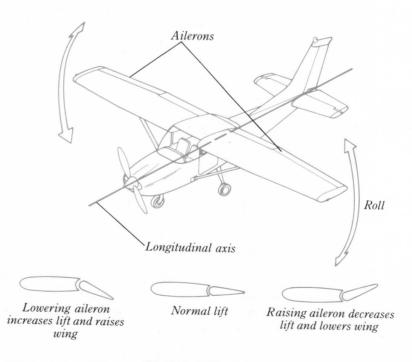

Ailerons

Roll

Longitudinal axis

Lowering aileron increases lift and raises wing

Normal lift

Raising aileron decreases lift and lowers wing

Figure 1-2. Ailerons

The elevators are movable control surfaces on the horizontal stabilizer at the rear of the plane (see Figure 1-3). They enable us to control the pitch of the nose, up or down, and thus our airspeed. Pressing your up-elevator key (go ahead and try it, just a single quick press) moves the elevators up, which forces the tail down and consequently the nose up. At your present speed, you will climb a bit. Conversely, pressing your down-elevator key once (go ahead and try it) moves the elevators back to neutral, which simultaneously brings the tail up and lowers the nose again. In your present configuration, you'll return to straight-and-level flight.

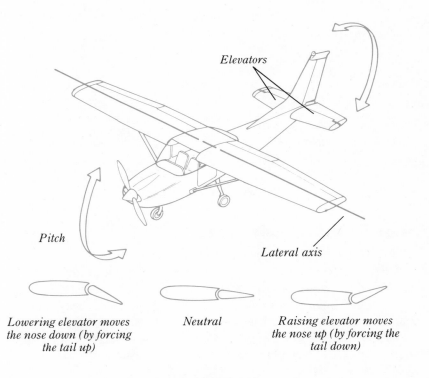

Elevators

Pitch

Lateral axis

Lowering elevator moves the nose down (by forcing the tail up)

Neutral

Raising elevator moves the nose up (by forcing the tail down)

Figure 1-3. Elevators

The primary purpose of the rudder is to counteract yaw—the tendency of the aircraft to turn on its vertical axis (see Figure 1-4). In coordinated flight, the rudder is set to the correct position automatically. Coordinated flight is the configuration you're in now.

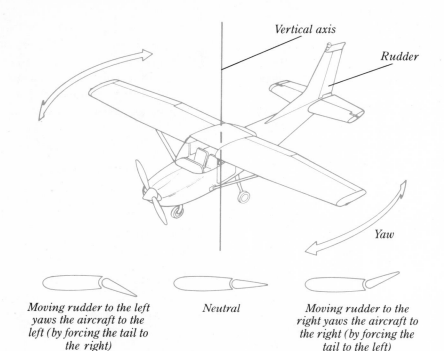

Moving rudder to the left yaws the aircraft to the left (by forcing the tail to the right)

Neutral

Moving rudder to the right yaws the aircraft to the right (by forcing the tail to the left)

Figure 1-4. Rudder

Omni-Bearing indicator

Omni-Bearing Indicators

Just to the right of the six primary instruments are two additional circular instruments. They're called Omni-Bearing Indicators, or OBIs for short. As the name implies, an OBI indicates your OMNI bearing, when and if you are within range of and tuned to a VOR (Very high-frequency Omnidirectional Range) transmitter. The uppermost OBI is equipped with a landing-approach aid called a glideslope. We won't use these instruments until we get into more advanced training in Section II of this book. At this point I just want you to know what they're called and where they are located.

Flaps, Trim, Throttle

To the right of the OBIs is a narrow column of indicators in what looks like a tube. From top to bottom, they are: flaps-position indicator, elevator-trim-position indicator, and throttle-position indicator. In the Piper there are blank spaces between them, and a mixture-control indicator is wedged in at the right of the throttle-position indicator.

Flaps are sections on the trailing, or rear, surface of the wings which can be lowered into the airstream to produce additional lift and, at the same time, drag (drag being a retarding effect, analogous to dragging your feet when someone is trying to carry you). They are used to shorten the distance required for takeoff, to descend at steeper angles without seriously increasing airspeed, and to enable slower speeds — particularly landing speeds — by decreasing the speed at which the wing will stall, or cease to have lift.

Elevator trim will not concern us, because we will use the elevator itself as the trim device.

You're already familiar with the throttle, but begin to think of it not as a speed control, but as an altitude control. Its primary purpose is for reaching and maintaining specific altitudes. You increase throttle to climb, reduce throttle to descend. In both cases, airspeed remains virtually constant.

Right now these indicators show that our flaps are up, or at zero degrees (the successively lower positions indicate 10, 20, 30, 40 degrees in Cessna and 10, 25, 40 degrees in Piper); the elevator trim is at neutral (actually, in the mode we fly, it's inoperative); and the throttle setting is at less than full power. The RPM indicator is more important to our flying technique than the throttle indicator, because it provides more exact information. In Piper, your fuel mixture (the ratio of fuel-to-air going through the carburetor and into the engine, where the vapors explode) is full rich. The full-rich setting will be standard for all our flights. Cessna, incidentally, has no mixture control, which is often the case in lightplanes.

Compass, Radio, Fuel/Oil, Mags, Gear

To the upper right of your panel you'll find the magnetic compass. In Piper it sticks out on top of everything and reads 332, as you would expect. In Cessna it's plainly labeled and reads 330. When it oscillates between two numbers, it simply means it hasn't settled down yet.

Just so you'll know (we'll learn more about these things when you're learning to navigate), the radio stack consists of six sections, all clearly named, if you'll look at them. The marker-beacon indicator has three lights reading O M I, for Outer, Middle, and Inner marker; they're used in instrument landings and indicate the distance from the runway. The COM or COM1, which stands for Communications radio, is used to contact airport towers and other aircraft. The two navigation radios, NAV1 and NAV2, are used to tune the aforementioned VOR stations. The distance-measuring-equipment readout, labeled DME, tells us our distance from any VOR we're in range of and tuned to. And the instrument with the four-digit code number labeled

Flap-position indicator

Elevator-trim indicator

Throttle-position indicator

Magnetic compass

Carburetor-heat indicator

Tachometer

TIME
12:00:00

Clock

XPNDR, which stands for Transponder (not Expander), is a transmitter on which ATC (Air Traffic Control) sometimes asks you to "squawk" to help them locate you. We won't be using the Transponder in this book, but at least you now know what and where it is. (Here in the World War I zone we're out of range of all communication and navigation aids, or I would have you turn something on just for the fun of it.)

Also amply labeled are the fuel gauges, showing the amount of fuel in your two gas tanks (one in each wing); the oil-temperature gauge, (C)old to (H)ot; the oil-pressure gauge, (L)ow to (H)igh; the MAGS or magneto-switch-position indicator, presently indicating (B)oth left and right magnetos on (magnetos are small AC generators used in the ignition system); the Lights indicator, reading ON or OFF/1 or 0. The Cessna panel also has an indicator for landing-gear position, UP or DN, which now reads DN, the default position, of course. The landing gear in Piper is fixed.

Look carefully at three more things on your panel and you'll have it all:

First, your carburetor-heat indicator, showing whether or not you've applied heat to the carburetor. In Cessna, it's at the bottom of the slot under your throttle indicator. In Piper, it's all the way over at the bottom right. When the reading is CH, your carburetor control is off—pushed all the way in. When it's red and reads HT, it's on—pulled all the way out. This control prevents your carburetor from icing up. On your first landing, in the "Greasing It On" chapter, you'll learn how to use it.

Second is your tachometer, which you've already worked with—the indicator with the readout labeled RPM. It's way at the bottom right in Cessna and to the left of the carb-heat indicator in Piper. This is one of the most important instruments we have, because it is our guide to power settings. It tells us how fast the engine, and the propeller connected to its crankshaft, are turning, in revolutions per minute (RPM). The propeller spins clockwise, incidentally, as viewed from the cockpit.

And finally, we have a digital clock, which keeps actual time, ticking off hours, minutes, and seconds—very accurately, you'll find, if you check it with your wristwatch.

Those scenics we've passed look just like the one we took off from, don't they? Even the river looks the same. But no matter how hard you stare, you can't see the runway. It was on this side of the river—remember?— and more or less in the righthand corner of the area, in relation to the way we're headed. If there were a runway there we'd spot it easily from this altitude. Well, that area down there is indeed the place we took off from—minus Eagle Field for some weird reason. We'll explore this phenomenon one day.

Before we end this flight, let's talk a little more about what we call "scanning." When we start flying in weather, you'll see why I emphasize this practice. If you develop the right habits as you learn, flying in weather will be a cinch for you—as will every other kind of flying.

Remember to scan your primary instruments, then the outside world, and occasionally (perhaps between every fifth or sixth primary scan) the other instruments and indicators. Don't just look, but mentally take note of each reading or indication, something like this:

"Airspeed: 115," or "130," or whatever you perceive it to be to the nearest ten knots, and as you get sharper, to the nearest five knots.

"Attitude: wings level. Pitch zero," referring to the white lines etched on the instrument. As you'll recall, the two lines in the center represent the wings of the aircraft, and the dot represents its nose. Each of the four short lines represents five degrees of pitch (nose up or down) in relation to the horizon. When the attitude indicator shows the horizon below your wings, you're pitched up; when above, you're pitched down; when right on, pitch is zero. If you were nose high, you might think "Pitch up one," meaning one five-degree mark; if nose low, "Pitch down a half," meaning half a mark, etc. You'll see what a bank looks like on the attitude indicator pretty soon.

"Altitude: 6700 and steady," or "6200 and descending"—whatever it reads. The large hand always reads hundreds of feet; the small hand reads thousands. And the independent little white marker (which we rarely use in normal flying) reads tens of thousands, so when it gets to the 1 you're at 10,000 feet, plus whatever thousands the small hand reads, plus whatever hundreds the big hand indicates. Don't be confused by the small hand, which reads thousands. When it's between numerals on the dial, read the lower numeral and multiply it by a thousand feet. Ignore the intermediate steps. Your big hand, remember, is reading the hundreds. (Did you notice, by the way, that you've lost some altitude lately? That kind of thing happens often when you're flying at what you think is a fixed altitude. Don't correct it now, but in our regular flying, make it your business to hold whatever cruise or other altitudes we decide on.)

Continuing your scan and readout:

"Rate of climb: Zero" or whatever it shows. The dial markings denote hundreds of feet per minute, with numerals only at 500, 1000, and 1500. So if the needle is on the first little mark above 5 you'll say "Rate of climb: 600" or "Climbing 600" or whatever is comfortable for you, as long as it tells you something and helps control what you're doing.

"Heading: 330" per the heading indicator.

"No bank. No turn." You're now looking at the turn coordinator. You can call it "the bank and turn" if you like, because it will tell you if one of your wings is lower than the other, which means you're in the bank, which means you'll turn in the direction of the low wing. So if your left wing were down, pointing in the vicinity of the L on the instrument, you would be turning left. On the other hand, if your right wing were down, pointing at the R, you'd be banking and turning to the right. It follows that you can just say "Level" when the turn coordinator indicates no bank, no turn.

The reason you don't scan the other instruments that relate to your flying condition—such as the compass, gauges, and tachometer (RPM)—with every revolution of your head is that they aren't likely to change as fast as the primary instruments. The magnetic compass will change if you change your heading, but your heading indicator will record that fact more quickly and reliably, since the compass takes a while to settle down. The RPM will change if you change power settings (the amount of throttle you are giving the engine) or if you go into a nosedive. Also, Piper RPMs will vary somewhat during descents. But for the most part, the RPM will remain where you set it.

You check the fuel, oil temperature, and oil pressure for signs of anything untoward. Running out of fuel before you reach your destination, for example, is what we call untoward. Or developing a gas or oil leak or having your oil temperature suddenly rise, indicating an overheated engine. (However, such things as leaks and overheating engines occur in the simulator only if you're flying Reality mode and have Reliability set to less than 100.)

If you're flying Piper, be aware that gas feeds from whichever tank the switch is set to, and the best idea is to switch regularly to balance the weight in the wings. Cessna does the dual feeding automatically.

You're coming along fine. But don't become so fascinated with your prowess at panel scanning that you ignore the world outside. Your eyes should check out front between passes over the panel. And very regularly, look out all sides of the aircraft; you never know what you might see—or miss. For example, you might miss the very airport you're headed for, or see a lake that shouldn't be there, or another of those mysterious Eagle Field scenics.

This ends your familiarization flight. Rest, if you need it, or continue to the next flight. Just press the Escape key to get back into the Editor.

Press the Editor key

Straight and Level

Eagle Field Training Base (Local)

**North: 17405. East: 7433. Altitude: 2000. Pitch: 0. Bank: 0.
Heading: 45. Airspeed: Cessna 114. Airspeed: Piper 122.
Throttle: Cessna 20479. Throttle: Piper 21463.
Rudder: 32767. Ailerons: 32767. Flaps: 0.
Elevators: Cessna 32767. Elevators: Piper 36863.
Time: 10:00. Season: 2. Clouds: 0.
Surface Wind: 4 kn., 270 deg.**

Whenever I refer to "straight and level," this is what I mean.

Look at all your instruments, and register what they're telling you. Out the windshield, notice how Eagle Field directly ahead of you becomes three-dimensional when you get close in. Flying Piper, you'll have just a last-minute glimpse of the hangar at the east end of Runway 27, because you're slightly nose high. In Cessna, you'll see the whole airport.

Your KIAS (Knots Indicated Airspeed) in Cessna is 104 nominal, but your actual airspeed is 114. It's important to remember this instrument discrepancy. You can regularly add eight to ten knots to the indicated airspeed in Cessna, and you'll have a more accurate figure. Your KIAS in Piper reads the correct value: 122 knots.

The artificial horizon exactly depicts your attitude in relation to the earth and sky. You are flying absolutely level in Cessna, which you can confirm by looking out all sides of the aircraft; the horizon is straight. In Piper, the nose of the airplane is pitched slightly up. (If you look out the right side from Piper, you'll see the slight apparent slant of the horizon, due to your nose-up configuration. This is perfectly normal.)

The altimeter confirms what we already know: steady at 2000 feet.

The VSI (Vertical Speed Indicator) reconfirms that you're neither climbing nor descending; gaining no altitude, losing none. Straight and level. (Note that frequently the VSI needle in Piper gets stuck at about 100 feet up. So you need more than this instrument to tell you that you're straight and level—for instance, a static altimeter indication.)

The heading indicator agrees with your compass: 45 degrees.

13

Press the Recall key

The turn coordinator shows your wings level: no bank, hence no turn.

Look at your RPM indication: 1905 in Cessna, 1950 in Piper. This power setting is what's required to cruise straight and level, at this altitude, on this particular spring day, with your elevators trimmed for operational neutral— 32767 in Cessna, 36863 in Piper.

To find or confirm, now or anytime, operational neutral in Cessna, temporarily apply one notch of forward pressure on the elevator. If it moves down from dead center, you were at operational neutral before you applied the notch of down pressure. So take off the notch and you're at neutral.

Piper's indication of operational neutral is when the elevator-position indicator sits just above the center mark but still touches it. If you give one notch of up trim and the position indicator moves up, you were at operational neutral before you applied the notch. Take it off and you return to neutral.

If you saved the flight parameters, press Recall to refly this demonstration until it feels as comfortable as an old pair of shoes. You'll spend more time in this configuration—straight and level—than in any other through all your flying. And, as easy as it looks, many students have more trouble flying like this than they do drawing beautiful sine waves all over the sky.

Standard Climbs and Descents

Eagle Field Training Base (Local)

**North: 17405. East: 7433. Altitude: 2000. Pitch: 0. Bank: 0.
Heading: 45. Airspeed: Cessna 114. Airspeed: Piper 122.
Throttle: Cessna 20479. Throttle: Piper 21463.
Rudder: 32767. Ailerons: 32767. Flaps: 0.
Elevators: Cessna 32767. Elevators: Piper 36863.
Time: 10:00. Season: 2. Clouds: 0.
Surface Wind: 4 kn., 270 deg.**

    The parameters specified above are the same parameters used in the previous flight, "Straight and Level." If you're already flying, just press Recall to start over again.

    If you're flying Cessna, increase your throttle setting two notches; if you're flying Piper, increase it three notches. Your tach will indicate 2105 RPM in Cessna, 2250 RPM in Piper.

    When your VSI settles down, you'll show a steady climb at 500 FPM.

    Continue the climb until your altimeter indicates 2700 feet, then press the Pause key and study your instrument panel.

    Your airspeed is not perceptibly different from when you were flying straight and level. Pitching up, as a result of increasing your power setting, has not slowed the airplane down. If anything, your airspeed has increased a knot or two, and keeping airspeed virtually constant is highly desirable.

    The artificial horizon confirms that you're pitched up approximately 2½ degrees from straight and level. The little abstract aircraft depicted on the face of the instrument is a half mark above the horizon. Thus the attitude indicated on the artificial horizon confirms what the rate of climb is reading: You're in a 500-FPM climb.

    Press the Pause key again to resume flying. Now the altimeter confirms what the artificial horizon and the VSI indicate: You're climbing.

    Take a view out the right side. In relation to your wing, the horizon has an apparent downward slant in the direction you're flying—indeed, to about the degree you would expect, hmm? That's something worth remembering: If, taking a look off the wing, the earth's horizon slants downward in the direction you're flying, you are climbing. If it slants upward, you're descending. It's

Press the Recall key

Press the Pause key

15

Press the Recall key

Press the Recall key

so logical, but someday when you're in trouble, you'll learn how easy it is to think illogically.

If you were flying in an overcast, with no outside references at all, you would still know that you were in a standard 500-FPM climb, wouldn't you? Everything on your instrument panel confirms the fact. Remember that.

And remember this: the 500-FPM climb is the most important climb you can have in your repertoire. It's the standard climb for instrument work and for VFR (Visual Flight Rules) flight, too.

Press your Recall key, returning to the straight-and-level configuration, and again set up a 500-FPM climb—i.e. add two notches to your present power setting for Cessna, three notches for Piper.

Your target altitude is, say, 2300 feet. When the hundreds needle of your altimeter shows you are one edge-mark (20 feet) below that altitude, take off the power you used for the climb—subtract two notches of throttle if flying Cessna, three notches if flying Piper.

Now watch your instruments. The airspeed varies slightly if at all. Your attitude as depicted on the artificial horizon resumes straight and level. The altimeter shows a residue of climb above the 2300 mark, but only briefly. Your VSI oscillates some (in Piper somewhat more than some), but then settles at its zero position. Your RPM is standard for straight and level in this altitude range, as before. And when everything settles down, look where your altimeter is—right where you targeted it when you made your power reduction: 2300 feet. That's precision flying.

So now whenever you're cruising straight and level, and want to climb to a higher altitude and then level off, you know exactly how to do it: In Cessna, increase your power setting two notches; in Piper, increase it three notches. Twenty feet below your desired altitude, decrease your throttle setting the same amount.

Now, press Recall, and return to the original straight and level configuration. This time Piper pilots get to see more of Eagle Field.

In Cessna, reduce your throttle setting two notches. In Piper, reduce it four notches. In both aircraft, this operational opposite of the 500-FPM climb procedure produces its counterpart: a 500-FPM descent. This is a standard-rate descent and the most important descent in your bag of tricks. Again, all the instruments and all your outside views confirm the fact that you're descending. Again, airspeed remains virtually constant, attitude is reflected in the artificial-horizon presentation (hopefully, in the case of Piper), the altimeter counterclocks the descent, the VSI confirms the rate, and everything is where it ought to be. (Note that in Piper the horizon off to your right is now flat, the 500-FPM descent offsetting the nose-up pitch you had while flying straight and level. Also note that the RPM indication in Piper is no longer an exact guide, as it normally is in Cessna, to power setting. The RPM varies in descents, though eventually the tachometer will read your actual RPM. However, the vagaries of the tach should not matter to you once you have the techniques we're working on fixed firmly in your mind.)

If you are currently below 1500 feet, press Recall, and repeat the throttle reduction described above, then read on. Otherwise, just read on.

Press the Recall key

When your altimeter indicates 1500 feet, add back the power you took off for your 500-FPM descent. The aircraft will gradually level itself, then begin a shallow climb.

Now why is it climbing? Our power and trim are at the same settings we used for straight-and-level flight. What's happening?

Well, the airplane is slowly climbing partly because—to put it as the British might—the *airscrew* has something more substantial to bite into. This altitude, or to put it more precisely, the density altitude in our immediate environment, finds the airplane in thicker air than at 2000 feet. This means a smidgin more thrust and lift, though the airspeed doesn't change. Changes in altitude, temperature, and moisture in the air, for example, change the density altitude, which affects the performance of the aircraft and often requires small control changes by us.

In the actual aircraft, we could correct for the present shallow climb with a smidgin less power or a smidgin of forward (down) trim on the elevators. But in the simulator, we have only an approximation of really fine control. Thus there's no way to make your Cessna or Piper fly straight and level for very long at just any random altitude without exercising some control. It will, however, fly straight and level for long stretches at certain specific altitudes, which it will choose for itself based on your power/elevator setting and the density altitude the simulator concocts from your weather and season parameters.

As you may have guessed, intermediate power settings—one instead of two ups or downs in Cessna, and one or two instead of three or four in Piper—will yield shallower rates of climb and descent. Use them when you want to gain or lose a little altitude and aren't in a hurry. But remember to return to your previous settings when you reach your target altitude.

So what about trim? If we leave our power setting where it is for straight and level, and trim the elevator to pitch up, won't we climb?

Let's see. Press Recall, and when things settle down we're back to straight and level at 2000, headed over good old Eagle Field. If you're flying Cessna, give two quick elevator notches up. If you're flying Piper, give one elevator notch up.

Press the Recall key

Sure enough, the nose pitches up. Then the VSI reads up, and then down, temporarily hitting about 1000 FPM, then 0 FPM, until it finally settles on a 500-FPM climb.

Press the Recall key

Meanwhile, what happened to our airspeed? There's nothing constant about it this time; all we did was trade airspeed for altitude.

What about up elevator plus a higher power setting? Let's see.

Press Recall, then when things settle down, add one notch of power and one notch of up elevator. This yields a climb of about 300 FPM in Cessna and, after considerable oscillation, 500 FPM in Piper.

So we can climb (and descend) with various combinations of power and elevator trim. But after exhaustive experimentation I can assure you that the most efficient and precise control of climbs, descents, and altitude itself is that resulting from specific power settings, with elevator trim only where it will hold a given altitude better than will power alone.

(It is certainly true that, in the actual aircraft, we could and would exert a little back pressure when we added power to climb. But such pressure would be less than is simulated by one notch of elevator in the plane you're flying and far less than is simulated by one notch of trim in Reality mode, which is one reason I find unReality in the simulator more real than Reality.)

And anyway, why use two operations to get a result we can get, smoothly and consistently every time, with one operation? Any aircraft, including your present Cessna or Piper, should be flown in the manner best suited to its design characteristics, rather than according to a generalized theory or the way some other airplane flies.

And it is a fact that, even in the actual aircraft, adding power while cruising straight and level will cause the plane to pitch up and climb, at a rate natural to its airfoil and the power applied. Similarly, a reduction of power will result in a pitch downward and a descent, under the smooth control of the engine all the time. For a simple aerodynamic reason: *Pitch follows power*.

Understanding how to fly power settings will help you immensely when we fly on instruments alone, as, for example, controlling altitude in an overcast or on an ILS (Instrument Landing System) approach. So, if you hang in there and pay careful attention, you'll wind up flying VFR, IFR, and ILS and everything else—except DOA—with precision.

Standard Turns

Eagle Field Training Base (Local)

North: 17408. East: 7422. Altitude: 2000. Pitch: 0.
Bank: 24. Heading: 180. Airspeed: 117.
Throttle: Cessna 20479. Throttle: Piper 21463.
Rudder: 32767. Ailerons: 32767. Flaps: 0.
Elevators: Cessna 33023. Elevators: Piper 37887.
Time: 11:30. Season: 2. Clouds: 0.
Surface Wind: 4 Kn., 270 deg.

As soon as the simulator settles down (it often takes two or three seconds for all the control interactions to get sorted out) note carefully the position of your right wing, as depicted on the turn coordinator, with respect to the little reference dot before the "R." The wing and the dot should line up.

I'm demonstrating a standard two-minute turn, the turn you'll virtually always use when flying IFR (Instrument Flight Rules, which means there is weather up there and you had better know what you are doing if you get into it). You will also use this kind of turn when flying an ILS approach, as well as in everyday flying when you want to make a nice leisurely turn. It's also called a "standard-rate turn."

"Two-minute turn" means that with this bank (averaging approximately 20 degrees) it will take your aircraft approximately two minutes to turn 360 degrees and, of course, one minute to reverse direction. We call the latter "doing a 180" for obvious reasons. The 180 is a very useful maneuver, for example: If you took off and flew a few miles and then remembered you left your briefcase in the hangar—or even worse, your lunch.

Now about the wing and the dot lining up on the turn coordinator display: They won't necessarily stay lined up, because the airplane tends to try to fly straight and level. But you want to be precise and keep it where it is. If the bank gets shallower, use right aileron to bring the wing back to the reference mark. Then as soon as it hits the mark, neutralize, by centering the control. Do this every time you notice in your scan that the bank has become shallower. Or if it steepens, use opposite aileron—in this case left aileron—whatever is necessary to hold the wing on the reference mark.

Note other things in relation to this turn: Your airspeed is quite steady. Your bank is depicted on the artificial horizon, agreeing with your out-the-windshield horizon. Pick some visible clue where one end or the other of the artificial horizon meets the edge of the instrument, so that you could execute a two-minute turn even if you had no bank-and-turn indicator. Note the lie of the real horizon with respect to your windshield. This is what a two-minute turn looks like.

Look again at your altitude indicator. Note that your nose is on the horizon, not below it. In combination with everything else you see, like the 2000 reading on your altimeter and the zero position of your VSI, your artificial horizon confirms that you are losing/gaining little or no altitude in the turn. And that's important.

A nice, precision, controlled level turn like this doesn't just happen. We're holding our altitude in the turn because we're holding a little back pressure on the yoke. To be exact, we are using one notch of up elevator as compared to operational neutral. You cranked in that notch when you set up the parameters for this flight. That's the only difference (other than right aileron) between this turn and straight-and-level flight. Your power setting, you'll note, is the same as it was when you were straight and level.

To experience the effect of failing to hold back pressure, even in a relatively shallow turn like this, apply a notch of down elevator. Keep your turn and bank steady. In Cessna you'll add 200–300 FPM on the down side. In Piper things go wild. The plane tries valiantly to right itself as the VSI nearly pins on 1500 FPM down and the airspeed indicator redlines. Imagine what it would be like if your bank were steeper; we'll experience that shortly.

So the rule is: On all but the shallowest and briefest turns, use back pressure—adding or subtracting it as needed—to hold your altitude. Eliminate whatever pressure you have applied as you roll out of the turn.

Speaking of rolling out, this is the ideal time to practice it. Press Recall to return to the standard two-minute turn we set up in the Editor. Fly for 10 or 15 seconds, keeping your wing on the reference dot and practicing your scanning. Then when you decide you're ready to fly straight, apply opposite aileron—the aileron opposite the direction of turn. As the airplane levels, take off the notch of back pressure and neutralize your aileron control.

Practice this for as long as you like. A good way to do it is, while you're turning, pick something on the landscape or horizon toward which you want to fly. Then try to time your rollout so that whatever you picked appears right ahead of you. Another idea is to decide on a compass heading you want to roll out on and practice it until you can nail it on the nose.

Press the Recall key

Practice the same turn to the left, too. I remember a pilot who used to fly at Totowa-Wayne who never departed the pattern. He would just rent a plane for an hour and fly the "box," shooting takeoffs and landings. Because we flew the usual lefthand pattern there, he became an absolute expert at banking and turning left. Then one day he took some dual with an instructor and found that he went completely haywire when he was asked to make a standard turn to the right. That's a true story. ("Taking dual" is slang for dual instruction, or flying lessons. All standard aircraft that seat two or more people have dual controls, so they can be flown from either the left or right seat. The instructor flies copilot in the right seat. Students, pilots, and airline captains habitually fly the left seat. And it can be amazing how your perspective changes when you change sides.)

Now I want to show you two additional turns which we'll regard as standard, and which we'll use when flying patterns and in various normal VFR flight situations.

Enter the Editor, press Recall to reset the original parameters for this chapter, and change just one value: Set Bank to 26 and press Return. Then exit the Editor. Note that this turn is a bit steeper than the two-minute turn. Note particularly the relationship of your wing and the dot. The wing is offset a bit below, rather than in line with the dot as in the 20-degree turn. For practical purposes, we'll call this a 25-degree bank and turn.

Make the same turn, this time to the left, relating your wing and the dot next to the L just as you did in the right turn.

Now enter the Editor again, press Recall, change the Bank parameter to 333, press Return, and exit the Editor. This is a 30-degree turn, in this case to the left. Note the attitude of your wing on the turn coordinator. Then apply a touch of right aileron, and note that the turn and bank "snaps" to the 25-degree indication. Stop it there by neutralizing the aileron. Once more use right aileron, this time to decrease the bank to the standard rate turn. Again it snaps in, and you can hold it there by neutralizing the control.

Experiment with banking, and get used to the look and feel of 20-, 25-, and 30-degree turns, left and right. Note that the steeper the bank, the longer it takes to roll out. Try perfecting your rollouts so that you anticipate them by 10, 15, and 20 degrees respectively when turning to a desired heading. The pattern-flying technique I'll show you shortly uses 25- and 30-degree turns in a very specific manner and you will have an easier time learning the technique if you have mastered the turns.

There's an even steeper "normal" bank you should be familiar with— the steepest that will register on your turn coordinator. It's a 35-degree bank, and you can see it by going into the Editor once more, pressing Recall, and changing the Bank parameter to 328.

Press the Editor key

Press the Recall key

In the steeper turns, by the way, you'll note that you're losing altitude, even though you have a notch of up trim. You can avoid this by adding a notch of power before you start your bank.

The smoothest turn performance, I find, results from applying back pressure (and for turns steeper than 25 degrees, power) before entering the bank. When rolling out, let off the back pressure (and power) after the wings are level. If you enter the turn before trimming or powering up a bit, your altitude starts slipping and it takes longer to re-establish balance. In any event, don't expect the VSI needle to cleave to zero throughout the maneuver. It will move around. You are turning, after all, in a medium much like water. If you see that you've lost altitude after the turn, use a notch of power to·climb back up, and vice versa if you've gained. Also don't forget that the vertical-speed indicator lags the actual performance of the aircraft. Keep in contact with your other instruments and with the landscape outside the windshield.

Don't worry if you don't make perfect turns and rollouts at the outset; all these things take practice. You have a lot to remember and do while you're flying. The real beauty of it all is the unmistakable challenge it offers us—to be sharp, to be always improving, to work on faults until we smooth them out, to execute something flawlessly even once, and gradually to become one with this superb machine that somehow, incredibly, gives us wings.

Climbing Turns

Eagle Field Training Base (Local)

**North: 17409. East: 7403. Altitude: 2054. Pitch: 0.
Bank: 338. Heading: 39. Airspeed: 120.
Throttle: Cessna 24575. Throttle: Piper 24576.
Rudder: 32767. Ailerons: 32767. Flaps: 0.
Elevators: Cessna 32767. Elevators: Piper 37887.
Time: 13:00. Season: 2. Clouds: 0.
Surface Wind: 4 kn., 270 deg.**

I have started a climbing turn to the left; this is what it's supposed to look like. Do your instrument scan and tell me what you see. Read out your airspeed, attitude, altitude, rate of climb, heading, and degree of bank.

Take the controls, and look out front. Don't worry about the mountain. You are about a mile from it, and if you don't let your bank get too shallow, you'll be fine.

And when all you can see is mountain out front, you still don't have to worry, because your instruments tell you what's happening.

We want to maintain a climb rate of about 500 FPM. If you're flying Cessna and it starts to slip below that, trim your elevator up a notch. Apply back pressure, just as in a level turn. If you're flying Piper, a notch of either up or down trim is too drastic. Try a notch of power one way or the other, and then a notch in the other direction to average as close to 500 FPM as you can. Hold the bank. Don't let it get too shallow.

In Cessna, too, if you need more than one notch of back pressure to hold the climb rate (you started the climb with neutral trim, whereas Piper started with a notch above neutral) add power. If the rate increases too much, let off some back pressure.

Line the left wing up with the dot, and keep it there. Work for a rate of climb of 500 FPM.

Climb like this to 3500 feet. Then roll out on a heading of 65 degrees.

Get straight-and-level heading 65, and clean up your altitude. I want you to be at 3500, plus or minus no more than 20 feet. Fly straight ahead, doing whatever you have to do to get it, but whether you get it or not, wake me up in about ten minutes and I'll show you my next trick.

23

Altitude Management

Eagle Field Training Base (Local)

**North: 17400. East: 7405. Altitude: 3484. Pitch: 0. Bank: 0.
Heading: 65. Airspeed: Cessna 121. Airspeed: Piper 125.
Throttle: Cessna 22527. Throttle: Piper 22528.
Rudder: 32767. Ailerons: 32767. Flaps: 0.
Elevators: Cessna 32511. Elevators: Piper 36863.
Time: 13:15. Season: 2. Clouds: 0.
Surface Wind: 4 kn., 270 deg.**

We learned earlier that these airplanes won't fly for long stretches at a given altitude, unless that altitude happens to suit them. But if we're going to fly like pros, we must fly the airplanes, not the other way around. There are several techniques I want to give you to help you maintain any altitude you select or are assigned.

If you're flying Cessna, one technique should be evident to you from your instrument scan. See if you can pick it out while I talk to Piper.

Piper, there is nothing unusual about what your aircraft is doing right now. You're very standard for the present density altitude. Your elevators are at operational neutral, and you're showing 2050 RPM, which is the optimum power setting for these conditions.

The trick, unfortunately, is holding this altitude, which is tougher for you than for Cessna—considerably tougher. Here's why: Cessna has 160 notches of elevator trim, compared to your 40. But that's not all. Each of Cessna's 160 notches changes the trim by a value of 256. Each of your 40 notches changes the trim by a value of 1024. A little math reveals that you both have the same range of elevator travel, but you have much less control over that travel. That's why you may go crazy in the sky when you use what you think is just a modest amount of trim, like one notch up or down. And that's why really precise control aloft eludes you.

Well, it needn't. The secret is: Use *power* to control your condition, and use elevator *very* sparingly. Manage your altitude with power. Correct for changes in altitude by putting on or taking off a notch of power. You'll find that you can hold within 20 feet of your present altitude, 3500, or any other altitude very nicely if you get the power habit. When you're about 20 feet below where

Press the Recall key

you want to be, add a notch of power and nose up to 20 feet over where you want to be. Then (isn't it lovely?) you can ease down for a full 40 feet before you have to repeat the procedure. How's that for mathematical wizardry?

While you're reading here, Recall the mode a few times. Try holding your altitude with elevator. Then start again, and try holding it with power. Do both a couple of times, and judge for yourself.

By the way, don't feel inferior to Cessna. Your throttle control, while it doesn't have the special half-steps that Cessna has, is very comparable in performance. Your engine sound is far superior (Cessna pilots can barely hear their engines unless they rig them with external amplification). And the squeal you hear when the rubber hits the runway is more satisfying than all of Cessna's sounds put together.

Cessna, see how nicely you hold your altitude? The reason is that you have 160 notches of trim to Piper's 40. At a specific altitude, you can usually use one notch of trim to stay straight and level if power doesn't do the job precisely. In the present situation, you're trimmed down one notch from operational neutral. That's what you noticed in particular when you did your scan, isn't it? And for the best result when you do use trim as an adjunct to power, let it be one notch, and let it be down trim. The reason it should be down rather than up is efficiency; you'll get better airspeed.

You have another advantage over Piper pilots, and that's the F6 on your input console. The F6 acts like a half notch of throttle. You can try it for holding altitude before you resort to trim. But remember, it's always a half-notch increase. There's no comparable decrease key. However, you can effect a half-notch decrease with one press of F6 and one press of F8, which will give you half the power reduction of F8 alone.

Slowflight/Normal Cruise Transition

Eagle Field Training Base (Local)

North: 17280. East: 7521. Altitude: 2000.
Pitch: Cessna 0. Pitch: Piper 359. Bank: 0.
Heading: 330. Airspeed: Cessna 80. Airspeed: Piper 84.
Throttle: Cessna 12287. Throttle: Piper 6144.
Rudder: 32767. Ailerons: 32767. Flaps: 0.
Elevators: Cessna 39679. Elevators: Piper 40959.
Time: 8:30. Season: 2. Cloud Layer 1: 10000, 7000.
Surface Wind: 3 kn., 330 deg.

Being able to "slowfly" the airplane is of great importance in your over-all proficiency. You should make the transition from normal flight to slowflight every time you approach an airport and when you fly an airport pattern. You'll make far better landings if you plan them from slowflight configurations. And slowflight is an absolute prerequisite for certain phases of instrument flying, such as during an ILS approach or when you're one of a "stack" waiting clearance to land.

You can regard your present configuration as standard for slowflight in your airplane, though it is possible to fly quite a bit slower than this.

Do your instrument scan thoroughly. In Cessna, you'll recall, your KIAS (Knots Indicated Airspeed) is lower by about ten knots than your instrument reading, so although you're indicating 70, you're doing about 80. In Piper you are reading 84. Note that your altimeter and your vertical-speed indicator both confirm that you're not losing or gaining altitude significantly. Note that your RPMs are lower than at cruise speed, too—1505 in Cessna, 1250 in Piper—so that to stay level you've had to trim the elevators up considerably.

Your exact throttle and elevator setting for slowflight will depend on your altitude when you make the transition. But as a general rule you'll reduce throttle by four notches in Cessna, seven notches in Piper. Then as the plane starts to descend, you'll trim the elevators up to hold your altitude. We'll practice this in a prescribed manner shortly.

But first, let's see how to transition from slowflight back to normal cruise. I'll describe it for each aircraft separately.

In Cessna, increase your throttle setting by four notches, for an RPM reading of 1905. Watch your VSI, and when it indicates about 400 FPM, apply two quick notches of down elevator. The VSI will indicate better than 500 FPM, then the needle will start down again, then up again, at which time give two more quick notches of down elevator. The VSI will indicate a descent briefly, then start to climb again. So, again apply two quick notches of down trim. The VSI will oscillate a bit, and then stop at the zero indication, and you'll be close to your original altitude. Your elevators will be at operational neutral. If you're more than 20 feet off your original altitude, add or subtract power briefly to restore the difference.

In Piper, increase your throttle setting by seven notches, for an RPM reading of 1950. Watch your VSI, and each time the needle flips up to indicate a climb, give one notch of down elevator, for a total of just four notches, which returns your elevators to operational neutral. The airplane will settle close to your original altitude. If you're more than 20 feet off, use power to correct.

You're now back to straight-and-level flight at your cruise speed and altitude, which is confirmed by both your instrument scan and your out-the-windshield views.

Transition to slowflight whenever you're ready. Here's how:

In Cessna, without rushing it, reduce your throttle setting four notches. Your RPMs will slow to 1505. Let the VSI needle indicate about 500 FPM down, then give two quick ups on your elevator. The VSI will swing to the up side, to about 500 FPM, then swing down again. When it indicates 500 FPM down, give two quick notches of up elevator. The VSI will go through the same oscillation. When it indicates close to 500 FPM down again, apply two final quick notches of up elevator. Then just wait. Things will settle down into the slowflight configuration you witnessed at the beginning of this flight. If your altitude is off a bit, again use one notch of power briefly—but no additional trim—to correct.

In Piper, without rushing things, reduce your throttle setting seven notches. Shortly, the VSI will indicate a descent of several hundred feet per minute. Counteract that with a notch of up elevator. Wait while the VSI swings up and then down again, and counteract with a second notch of up elevator. Repeat this procedure for two more—or a total of four—notches and then wait. You'll settle into the slowflight configuration that began this flight. If your altitude is off a bit, use a notch of power briefly—but no additional trim—to correct.

Press the Recall key

I recommend you use the Recall key to practice these transitions—from slowflight to normal cruise to slowflight—several times. With experience, you'll get a feel for when to execute your trim for the smoothest possible transition. But remember, whichever way you're transitioning, make your power change first; use elevator to get the desired result.

It's possible, certainly, to make smoother transitions than I've described here—if you have all the time in the world to make them. But these are speedy and efficient, use specific parameters you can rely on as standard, and hold your altitude within very reasonable limits.

By now you've probably had about all the practice you can take, learned all the techniques demonstrated, and are itching to fly and try everything for yourself under normal flying conditions.

Well, you should have sufficient basic flying skill now to take instruction in the air. So from here on out, you'll do the flying—all the way.

Preflight, Taxi, Takeoff, Turns

Eagle Field Training Base (Local)

**North: 17417. East: 7448: Altitude: 410. Pitch: 0. Bank: 0.
Heading: 22. Airspeed: 0. Throttle: 0. Rudder: 32767.
Ailerons: 32767. Flaps: 0. Elevators: 32767. Time: 14:00.
Season: 2. Clouds: 0. Surface Wind: 3 kn., 270 deg.**

Check your heading just to be sure the simulator has pointed you 22 degrees. If not, press the Recall key.

This is where the airplane is usually parked at Eagle Field, close by the east end of the hangar. The last person to fly the plane always leaves it here, so the next person knows where to find it. This is where we'll put it when we come back from a flight, unless we're the last pilots of the day, in which case we'll put it in the hangar.

Directly ahead outside your windshield is the last foothill of the mountains that rim this area to the north. Look out your left side, through the hangar, and you'll see another mountain range, with an arrow shape painted on the rocks halfway up. Those mountains border the whole area to the west. A left rear view would show you the rest of them, but the hangar is in the way. One mountain peak, which you can't see from here, is snowcapped.

It's important to familiarize yourself with all landmarks in the area of an airport, because they can help you get your bearings aloft.

Go into radar and take the highest view that still shows the hangar in detail. Your airplane is pointed toward Runway 9/27. We number runways this way because each strip is actually two runways, since you can take off and land in either direction. The numbers correspond to compass headings, but with the zeros dropped, for example: Runway 27 here at Eagle bears 270 degrees, or due west, while its reciprocal, Runway 9, points due east. In aviation language, the reciprocal of any heading is its exact opposite—that heading plus or minus 180 degrees. Sometimes we "do a 180" to get out of weather or other trouble. In Piper, your heading indicator automatically reads out the reciprocal of whatever heading you're on. In Cessna you don't have that luxury. In both planes you can (though you shouldn't have to) find a reciprocal by setting a given heading on your OBI. We'll cover operation of the OBI when we get into navigation technique.

Runways are usually designed to take advantage of the prevailing winds in the area of an airport. The prevailing winds here at Eagle are from the west, so 27 is the runway we'll use most often. The runway in use at any given time is called "the active runway" or just "the active."

Major metropolitan airports like JFK in New York and O'Hare in Chicago have up to a half dozen or more strips. JFK has five strips, which means ten runways. O'Hare has seven, for a maze of 14 different runways. All these runways consider the wind direction, as well as other factors, including traffic. Twelve of O'Hare's, for example, are in pairs, each of which faces the winds that prevail around the Windy City.

When two runways are on the same compass heading, a Right or Left is added to their number. Thus O'Hare has a 32 Right and a 32 Left, designating the way they lie as viewed by a pilot planning to land on one of them. Of course Left and Right trade places when the wind shifts: Runway 32R becomes Runway 14L, and 32L reciprocates by becoming 14R.

Another thing you should know about runways at large airports is that the shortest and narrowest are most often, though not always, used by lightplanes like ours. Relegating the behemoths to the big strips keeps them out of the way of planes that have more important places to go, like ours.

I want you to be serious about your flying. So before we fly I want you to understand how we know this airplane is airworthy. The first thing we do before we ever climb aboard is perform a preflight check. Here are the kinds of things we check:

Condition of tires. Brake lines for leaks. Fuselage, particularly around the landing gear, for wrinkles or signs of stress. Fuel, by feeling the gas in the wing with our fingers (we don't rely on gauges; we get a ladder or a box to stand on if we have to, so we know for sure that we have two full tanks of fuel). We also drain a little fuel into a jar or glass and check it to be sure it's clear and that there's no water in it.

We open the engine cowling on the pilot's side and check the left magneto switch and ground wires for looseness or fraying. We look for cracks in the carburetor and cabin heat shrouds. We drain some more fuel, this time from the strainer near the firewall, and check for contaminants. If everything looks right, we close the left cowling and secure it.

We inspect the static-system vent and Pitot tube to be sure no insects or other foreign bodies are blocking it, which could foul up our altimeter, rate of climb, and airspeed indicators. We check the prop for nicks and to be sure the hub nuts are safetied, and we look into the engine-cooling openings behind the prop for anything that shouldn't be there (birds or their nests, stray cats, remains of a ham on rye, etc.). We check the carburetor-intake screen and oil radiator for damage or obstructions.

On the right side of the engine we open the cowling, check the ignition leads and the right magneto, check the oil and secure its cap, and take another long look. As my first flight instructor, Arnold Kufta, used to say, "you're looking for anything unusual," though of course it all looked unusual to me. If everything seems to be in place, we close and secure the cowling.

We inspect the landing-gear strut fittings to be sure they are safetied. Then we examine the undersides of both wings for any signs of stress or damage, and the strut attachments to be sure they are safetied. We manually move the ailerons up and down, checking for any slackness or friction while we inspect the hinges. We operate the elevators, again manually, checking for full travel and for safetying of the hinge bolts. We check top and bottom surfaces for wrinkles and other signs of stress. We move the rudder back and forth, making sure it has unobstructed travel. On each wing of the airplane we check the flap hinges for cracks and excessive wear.

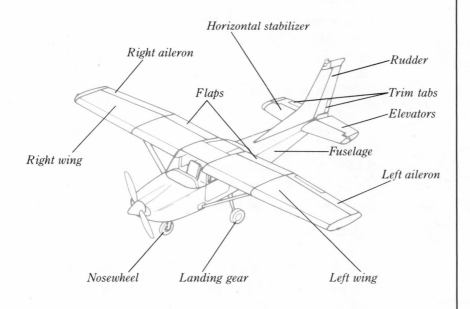

Figure 8-1. Basic aircraft components

If, based on our preflight inspection, everything looks okay, we climb in the airplane. If not, we don't. When we do climb aboard, with all the foregoing checks, inspections, and information in our heads, we know for sure that the airplane will fly.

Once in the cockpit, here's a checklist of jobs you should perform: (A bracketed R after an item means it is significant only in Reality mode, and then—except for trueing directional gyro and altimeter—only if Reliability is set to less than 100. You should be aware that all these checks are essential when flying an actual aircraft.)

1. Check carburetor-heat off. The last person who flew the airplane, including you, may have left it pulled out after landing. (In the actual airplane, carb heat is a push-pull control.)

2. Start your engine [R]. Your magneto switch is set to both, the battery master switch is turned on, and the starter is engaged. (The propeller turns clockwise as seen from the cockpit.)

3. Check magnetos [R]. Make sure your left and right magnetos are operating, then switch back to both.

4. Check oil temperature and oil pressure. Both gauges should read near their centers.

5. Check lights. In the daytime, you don't need running or instrument lights. Check the lights indicator on the right edge of your panel, and if they're on, turn them off. (If your readout is digital, 1 means on, 0 means off.)

6. Set directional gyro [R] when your magnetic compass settles down.

7. Set altimeter [R] to the current barometric pressure. In flight, reset it every 15 or 20 minutes to assure accuracy.

Before we start to taxi, perform the following takeoff preparations:

1. Check carb heat off. Make this part of your preparation for every flight, or you'll find your aircraft's performance is not at all what you're expecting.

2. Put on 10 degrees of flaps. That will be standard for all our takeoffs.

3. Be sure that your elevator is at its center position. (It will be if you set the Elevators parameter at 32767 in the Editor; but if you've been flying and are going to take off again without returning to the Editor, use the procedure described in the "Straight and Level" flight. Remember that in Piper center position is not "operational neutral.")

4. Apply two quick notches of up elevator. (This is analogous
to setting takeoff trim in the aircraft.)

Every time I tell you something like "get ready for takeoff," I expect you
to go through the takeoff preparation checklist. If you take off without going
through the four steps above, we won't be talking the same language.

Now we'll taxi along the tarmac to Runway 27. Use enough power to get
the airplane moving. Two notches are needed in Cessna; one in Piper. But
coast shortly after you get moving, because the last turn onto the runway is a
sharp one. While taxiing, if we were flying an actual aircraft, we would operate our ailerons, elevators, and flaps, checking them visually out the windshield to the left and rear. But you can't see any of these things from where
you are sitting, so I'll excuse you. (We would also stop short of the active,
turn into the wind, do the magneto checks described earlier, and run the engine up to be sure we had takeoff power, followed by proper idle on closing the
throttle. But the simulator brakes won't hold well enough to let us do that.)

In an actual plane, by the way, you would be steering with your feet, because your left and right rudder controls would be on the floor.

Follow the tarmac, and use radar if it helps, to get to 27. Go back and try
again if you have problems. Piper is much harder to steer than Cessna; you
have to anticipate your turns, watching out front and applying small amounts
of left or right pressure, then immediately neutralizing to avoid overcontrol.

Once you're on the runway, keep going. Don't stop or try to put the nose
of the plane precisely on the center line, but steer as you roll, trying to get
and keep the far end of the runway at the center of your windshield. Even if
you roll onto the grass, it's not the end of the world. Just steer back to the runway, and work to get the far end of it straight ahead of you.

When you're reasonably lined up, smoothly put on all your power.
(Never use the shortcut the manual suggests for instant full throttle or instant
full cut. Never. All power settings should be arrived at smoothly.)

Watch your airspeed. When it indicates 80 knots, rotate, using one press
of up elevator. You'll see the moment of rotation out your windshield.

Now pay attention to your VSI. As soon as it indicates a climb (it'll lag the
actual liftoff), give one press of down elevator. This lets off the back pressure
you used to rotate.

Dump your flaps (set them back to 0 degrees).

Wait while your VSI swings down and starts back up. When it indicates
about 1000 FPM up, take off the rest of your trim: Cessna, use two quick
notches of down elevator; Piper, use one notch of down elevator.

Now slowly reduce your power in Cessna by four notches (to 2105 RPM)
and in Piper by two notches (to 2250 RPM), applying each notch when the VSI
needle is moving up. You'll settle in a 500-FPM climb at better than 100 KIAS
with your elevators at operational neutral.

Keep climbing straight out. Notice the snowcapped peak over to your left and the shape directly ahead, an abandoned airport named Wigwam.

When your altitude is 2000 feet, start a standard rate turn to the left, rolling out on a heading of 180. If you do this well, you'll be flying along side the mountain range and a mile or so east of it. (The grid lines on the ground lie north/south and east/west and mark off square miles.)

Get straight and level at 2500. This simply requires, if you have done everything right so far, a power reduction about 20 feet below your target altitude: in Cessna, reduce two notches, for an RPM reading of 1905; in Piper, reduce three notches, for an RPM reading of 1950. If you recall, that's the procedure we learned in the "Standard Climbs and Descents" flight. See how everything get's integrated?

When the last grid line disappears under your nose, give me a standard-rate left turn to a heading of 90 degrees. Don't forget to precede the bank with a notch of back pressure, as you learned when you practiced turns. Then take that pressure off when you've completed the turn. You'll be flying east along the southernmost line of grids. Take all your left side views and admire the river and landscape.

Again, as the final grid line disappears, apply a notch of back pressure and turn left to head 360 degrees (i.e. 0), due north. Don't forget to take off the notch of pressure when you level the wings. Procedures like these, if you always do them the same way, will become habitual. You'll soon do them instinctively, which is what we want.

Now get into slowflight. If you don't remember how to do this, press the Pause key and review the "Slowflight" chapter beginning on page 26.

When the base of the mountain is even with the bottom of your windshield, turn right to a heading of 90 degrees, using the notch of back pressure (as usual) before you bank and take it off after you're level. Remember to start your rollout when you're about ten degrees from the heading you want.

Once you're in slowflight, level and headed 90 degrees, exit to the Editor and set up the parameters for your next flight. I'll show you how to transition from straight-and-level slowflight to a final approach and landing.

Press the Pause key

Greasing It On

Eagle Field Training Base (Local)

**North: 17418. East: 7458. Altitude: 1300.
Pitch: Cessna 0. Pitch: Piper 359. Bank: 0. Heading: 269.
Airspeed: Cessna 80. Airspeed: Piper 84.
Throttle: Cessna 12287. Throttle: Piper 6144.
Rudder: 32767. Ailerons: 32767. Flaps: 0.
Elevators: Cessna 39679. Elevators: Piper 40959.
Time: 15:00. Season: 2. Clouds: 0.
Surface Wind: 3 kn., 330 deg.**

NOTE: Before you exit to fly this approach and landing, read the narration below several times to familiarize yourself with the operations described.

You know how to slowfly the airplane. You were doing it when you departed the last flight. If you went directly into Editor at that point and your slowflight procedure was correct, you would have changed just altitude and heading to set up the parameters for this chapter. In fact, had you flown out some distance, lost some altitude and done a 180, you would have arrived at just about the position you are in now. However, I wanted to line you up for the runway this time, so you could concentrate on procedure rather than directional control.

You're on a straight-in approach to Runway 27 at Eagle Field, the runway from which we took off earlier. From here you can see the snowcapped mountain and the arrow painted halfway up the other peak. The arrow tells you are on the right heading, because (as I hope you remember) it is visible on the right front of your windshield when you're on the runway.

We're at pattern altitude, 1300 feet, a little more than a mile from touchdown. Pattern altitude—the altitude at which we're supposed to fly in the vicinity of any airport—is 800 to 1000 feet AGL (Above Ground Level). Since the elevation at Eagle Field is 410 feet, operations there call for a pattern altitude of 1210 to 1410 feet. In practice, we use 1300 feet.

Here is the technique for transitioning from pattern airspeed to a controlled descent, landing approach, flare, and touchdown. ("3-D" refers to the point at which the hangar takes dimensional shape.) Start as soon as you exit the Editor. For purposes of this flight, follow the prescribed procedure exactly. Don't change the direction of the flight, even though you may touch down or roll out on the grass. Don't take any actions other than those described under "Technique" below. What I want you to do here is to *see* what our standard landing approach should look like.

Cessna Technique:

1. Put on carb heat.
2. Extend flaps one notch.
3. On 500 FPM descent, reduce throttle two notches.
4. On 3-D, trim elevator down two quick notches.
5. Full flaps.
6. At 500 feet altitude, trim elevator up two quick notches.
7. At 430 feet altitude, trim elevator up two quick notches.
8. Continue gradual back pressure to touchdown.

Piper Technique:

1. Put on carb heat.
2. Extend flaps one notch.
3. On 500 FPM descent, reduce throttle one notch.
4. On 3-D, trim elevator two quick notches down.
5. Full flaps.
6. At 550 feet altitude, trim elevator up one notch.
7. At 450 feet altitude, trim elevator up one notch.
8. Continue gradual back pressure to touchdown.

If you've had trouble landing your airplane well, or you're just learning how to fly, the technique outlined above should help you considerably. I suggest you use Recall a number of times—maybe a hundred times—and practice this approach until it feels comfortable and natural. Then come back to it and fly it some more whenever you feel yourself getting rusty.

Press the Recall key

This approach gives you several things to think about. You got into landing configuration from slowflight configuration. You were at pattern airspeed and pattern altitude just before you put on your carb heat and your first notch of flaps. The same holds true in approaching any airport from any direction. In this case, you were making a straight-in approach. However, had you been "flying the pattern," (flying a rectangular series of takeoffs and "touch-and-go" landings—a typical practice routine), you would be straight and level on the downwind leg, and your landing technique would follow the same procedure. You would put on carb heat and a notch of flaps (Technique steps 1 and 2) when opposite your landing point. You would reduce your power (Technique step 3) after "turning base" (making your next-to-last turn before your final approach). After (or sometimes while) turning final, you would get into final-approach configuration (Technique steps 4 and 5). Then you would judge when to decrease your rate of descent a bit with up elevator (Technique step 6) based on your altitude and your relationship to the runway. And to flare and land (Technique steps 7 and 8), you would again be using your eyes, your judgment, and your skills to make as good a landing as possible.

All of the foregoing applies equally to entering an airport pattern, which officially should be done at a 45-degree angle to the downwind leg. You would be at pattern airspeed and altitude as you entered, and the rest of the procedure would be the same.

In our future flights you'll have many opportunities to practice this technique in many different situations. Every landing, however, is unique. You'll rarely make a perfect one, but before long you'll regularly make good ones. And if you foul up once in a while, welcome to the group. At least, if you follow the technique, you'll know what you did wrong—which, in the case of landings, usually means what you did too late or too early.

One last word: By "follow the technique" I mean apply its basic principles every time you land—follow the exact throttle, trim, and flap procedure, and settings given, the only judgmental aspect of it all being when to perform each operation. That's the fun part.

Ground Effect

Eagle Field Training Base (Local)

**North: 17412. East: 7438. Altitude: 520. Pitch: 0. Bank: 0.
Heading: 63. Airspeed: Cessna 114. Airspeed: Piper 122.
Throttle: Cessna 20479. Throttle: Piper 19415.
Rudder: 32767. Ailerons: 32767. Flaps: 0.
Elevators: Cessna 32255. Elevators: Piper 36863.
Time: 16:00. Season: 2. Clouds: 0.
Surface Wind: 0 kn., 0 deg.**

Press the Editor key

Press the Recall key

Don't tell anybody I did this; I just thought you might need a little relief from all this heavy concentration. Look back after the pass, and watch everything recede. Fly it a couple of times.

How high do you suppose that thing actually sits off the ground?

Let's see if we can find out. Go into the Editor, press Recall, then set Slew to 1, North Position to 17417, and East Position to 7447.

Now exit the Editor. Using Heading Slew, turn right to point 90 degrees. You should be looking straight across the hangar roof. And you're suspended over it, 110 feet off the ground (the elevation at Eagle, remember, is 410 feet).

Now switch your view in the normal way to look directly down at the tarmac below your wheels. Then carefully slew east, and stop slewing when you see all white roof.

Return to your out-of-the-windshield view. Take views to all sides, if you like—they're a bit unusual.

Next, slew a bit further east, comparing front and rear views to get at the approximate center of the roof.

Then, very carefully, use the Altitude down slew (Cessna use the F8 key) to try to put your aircraft atop the hangar. Then we'll be able to determine its height off the ground.

Flying the Pattern

Eagle Field Training Base (Local)

**North: 17418. East: 7449. Altitude: 410. Pitch: 0. Bank: 0.
Heading: 250. Airspeed: 0. Throttle: 0. Rudder: 32767.
Elevators: 32767. Time: 7:30. Season: 2. Clouds: 0.
Surface Wind: 6 kn., 270 deg.**

This will be your last regular training session here at Eagle Field before we go out into the big world, but it's an important one.

You're going to learn how to fly an airport pattern—something you'll do often for takeoff and landing practice, as well as for familiarizing yourself with the locale of a strange airport. And just for the fun of it on Sunday afternoons.

The idea of taking off, flying a rectangular route around an airport, and landing again may seem like the simplest of procedures. It isn't. In fact, it's one of the most difficult and challenging bits of airwork you'll ever undertake. In terms of actually handling the airplane, if you can fly a pattern well you're on your way to becoming a genuine expert. And believe me, pattern flying is tougher in the simulator than it is in the prototype.

I'm going to talk you through the entire procedure here, and I don't expect you to get it down pat the first time around. You will find, however, that like everything else in flying, practicing—in this case your pattern technique—will get you the rewards you want.

Get ready for your takeoff now. The procedure bears repeating: 1) check carb heat off; 2) trim for takeoff with two quick notches up; 3) put on 10 degrees of flaps.

We're using Runway 27, the threshold of which is directly ahead. Taxi forward at your own speed, keep moving, line up with the far end of the runway, and smoothly apply full throttle.

Rotate with one notch of back pressure at 80 KIAS. Let the pressure off again as soon as your VSI indicates a climb. Then when you're climbing at least 500 FPM, dump your flaps. But don't trim the nose down as you do when departing a pattern. We want a faster climb and a lower airspeed.

After your flaps are off, Cessna, reduce your throttle four notches to 2105 RPM; Piper, reduce two notches to 2250 RPM.

At 900 feet, without your customary notch of back pressure, bank left and enter a 30-degree turn (that calls for your next-to-steepest indicated bank, remember). Start your rollout when heading about 200 degrees, bringing the wings of the aircraft level on the crosswind leg, 180 degrees. Cessna, reduce your power two notches for 1905 RPM. Piper, reduce your power three notches for 1950 RPM.

Climb just briefly, to 1200 feet, and again with no back pressure enter another 30-degree turn to the left. Start your rollout when you're heading about 110 degrees, anticipating the downwind heading of 90 degrees.

Once downwind you should be at or close to pattern altitude, 1300 feet. Now transition to slowflight, but compress the operation as follows:

- Cessna, reduce your throttle four notches (1505 RPM).
- Piper, reduce your throttle seven notches (1200 RPM).
- Cessna, give two quick notches up elevator.
- Piper, give one notch up elevator.
- Cessna, give two more quick notches up elevator.
- Piper, give two slow (separated by about a second) notches up elevator.

At this point—if all went well—you'll be in standard slowflight configuration when things settle down. But don't wait for them to settle down.

Take a view of the runway out your left window, and from this point on keep the runway more or less in sight (or in your mind when it is obscured by the wing) all the way through to the landing.

Opposite the end of the runway where you're going to touch down, put on carburetor heat, followed by 10 degrees of flaps.

Keep your side view. A few seconds after the runway disappears, check the turn coordinator, and enter the 25-degree bank—the one that puts your wing just below the dot. Check the instrument frequently and hold that bank.

As the runway crosses your screen, switch to a 45-degree view, anticipating its reappearance, and be ready to start your rollout 15 degrees ahead of your base-leg heading, which is 0 degrees. So you'll start leveling off when heading 15 degrees.

As soon as you level your wings on base leg, Cessna reduce your power setting by two notches; Piper by one notch.

Right away, start another 25-degree turn, this time to final approach. Alter this bank as needed to keep the runway at an angle—but an ever-diminishing one—as it moves across your view. If it looks as if it will straighten out by the time it's about three-quarters of the way across your 45-degree-view screen, steepen the bank; if not, hold it—or if the angle appears too great, use a little opposite aileron to shallow the turn a bit.

Switch to your out-front view in anticipation of the runway reappearing, and then roll out at the rate which best lines you up for final approach.

Before you exercise any additional directional control, apply two quick notches of down elevator, and put on all your flaps.

Now use some — but not all — of your remaining altitude to get lined up. As in your landing-practice session, you'll want to start leveling off — Cessna with two quick notches up at about 500 feet, Piper with one up at about 550 feet. At that point you are committed direction-wise. Land on the grass, if need be, but don't start wagging your wings a few feet above the ground.

Cessna, flare with two quick notches of up elevator about 20 feet off the deck. Piper, flare with one notch up about 40 feet off the deck. Then use gradual back pressure to keep the airplane flying a foot or so off the ground as long as you can. If you get a stall warning at the moment of touchdown, you landed perfectly. If the warning sounds before touchdown, correct with one notch of forward pressure.

You'll want to practice flying the pattern here at Eagle Field and at your favorite airports often as you perfect your slowflight, approach, and landing techniques. The thing about Eagle Field is that it's very demanding; the challenge is to prevent the runway and hangar from becoming two-dimensional lines, which they will if you extend your crosswind or downwind legs too far. The airport should remain three-dimensional throughout the pattern (you won't be fined if it doesn't, but there's a great satisfaction if you maintain the realism. And with the expertise you gain as a result, flying into other simulator airports will be a cinch).

Will you always have to know exactly at what altitude you're to turn to each leg when you're pattern-flying at other airports? No. After some practice, you'll have a feel for it, and it'll become automatic, like the rhythm of turning a car around a corner or hitting a golf ball.

But you will have to be aware of the headings of the various legs of the pattern. Otherwise you'll find yourself way out of line. Remember that all turns are 90-degree turns, so in left-hand traffic patterns you subtract 90 degrees from the heading for each leg to determine the heading for the next. In right-hand patterns you will add 90 degrees to each leg. The compass roses provided in your manual will help you visualize these turns, and you should have the chart of the area you're flying open on your flight desk anyway to use. It's particularly helpful to refer to a compass rose when the legs of the pattern take you through the 0-, or 360-degree, heading. More helpful still is a pad, with the legs you need to fly and the pattern altitude jotted down for instant reference. A pen and a pad are two important flight instruments. Don't leave the runway without them.

Press the Save key

One other thing: Don't get upset if your heading on one or more legs is off by a few degrees. The procedure is infinitely more important than the precise heading. If you spend a lot of time trying to correct for a few degrees, your altitude or airspeed or something else is likely to suffer.

I put your airplane close to Runway 27 as a practice convenience. If I were you, I'd save this mode on disk and fly it often. The challenge of keeping the airport three-dimensional offers just about ideal practice conditions. And it's the only airport in the whole simulator world (at least for the present) that has a three-dimensional reference—the hangar—right alongside the runway; thus I find it the most realistic as well as the most colorful airport of them all. It's only drawback is that, if you're flying Piper, it doesn't recognize such things as dusk, night, or dawn. If you're flying Cessna, however, don't miss the incredible, other-worldly scenics of non-daytime pattern flying here. Use the present mode, and just change the time to a wee hour, like 23:00 for night or 6:00 (in springtime) for dawn. It's lavish.

SECTION 2
NAVIGATION
AND
Instrument Flying

Big Wheels

Tweed-New Haven Muni, CT to Boston Logan, MA

North: 17346. East: 21322. Altitude: 13. Pitch: 0. Bank: 0. Heading: 220. Airspeed: 0. Throttle: 0. Rudder: 32767. Ailerons: 32767. Flaps: 0. Elevators: 32767. Time: 5:40. Season: 3. Cloud Layer 1: 3500, 2000. Surface Wind: 5 kn., 190 deg.

Why do I start a flight like this at daybreak? It's not because I like getting up in the middle of the night. It's so that no matter how lost we get, we'll surely arrive where we're going by cocktail time, twelve hours from now, which I don't intend to miss.

Your going to learn a great deal today: including how to fly in and over weather and how to use your NAV (for NAVigation) radio to fly OMNI radials.

Before we take off, go into radar and zoom out until you can see a strip of land to your left across the water. The land is Long Island, and the water you'll take off over is Long Island Sound. The notch of water to your right is New Haven Harbor. Across the harbor is West Haven, and at the top of the notch is New Haven, Connecticut, home of Yale University. New Haven was a seaport in colonial days. And it might interest you to know that in 1883 there was a bewitched house on Church Street with sounds of tramping feet and objects flying around. A sick woman was stirring a cup of medicine and the spoon flew away. Then apparently something shot at at her, because there was a bullet hole in a window. But no bullet was ever found in the house.

The highway you see is Interstate 91. Switch to the out-front view, and get ready for your takeoff on Runway 20 (ahead of you, as you can see).

Put on your power and roll whenever you're ready. Make your regular departure takeoff and climb-out—rotate at 80 KIAS (one notch of back pressure, which you ease off again as soon as the VSI indicates a climb), dump your flaps when you're climbing better than 500 FPM, flatten the climb with two quick presses of down elevator in Cessna and one press in Piper, followed by a four-notch power reduction to 2105 RPM in Cessna, and a two-notch power reduction to 2250 RPM in Piper.

See how easy it is? You're soon climbing at 500 FPM. (By the way, the only difference between the departure takeoff and climb-out, and the technique you use when flying a pattern, is the flattening of the climb. When you're going to fly a pattern, keep the climb steeper and the airspeed slower, so that it's easier to transition to straight and level at pattern airspeed.)

44

Climb straight on out until you're in the overcast (bottoms are at 2000 feet). Long Island will become visible on your way up.

Level off at 2200 feet, using a power reduction of two notches for 1905 RPM in Cessna, and three notches for 1950 RPM in Piper. Make the reduction when the altimeter reads about 20 feet (one mark) under 2200. Don't touch your elevators.

Now consider: You're not flying "blind" in this overcast. You know exactly what you're doing. Everything is under absolute control. Your airspeed is right where it ought to be. Your attitude is level on the horizon. Your altimeter confirms that you are straight and level at 2200. You're not climbing or descending, and your Vertical Speed Indicator says the same. Your heading is what it was when you took off—within a degree or so of 200. Your turn indicator shows no bank, no turn. You are straight and level. Who needs the outside world when you have all those references right in front of you?

Now, as you fly, tune your NAV1 radio to a frequency of 110.0. If you don't know how to do this, use the Pause key and look at the directions in your manual. Then press the Pause key again to resume flying, and tune in 110.0.

Now check your DME reading. It's somewhere in the vicinity of 50. Is the number increasing or decreasing?

So now you know that whatever VOR station I had you tune to, your present heading is taking you where—away from, or toward it?

The VOR station, or OMNI, can be visualized as a big wheel with 180 spokes radiating from its hub. In the simulator the spokes are spaced two degrees apart, spanning a complete 360-degree circle. The wheel does not turn; it is you and your aircraft that are moving. You are somewhere in relation to one or two of the spokes of the wheel, moving like a spider on a web, straight out along a spoke or strand, or diagonally between two of them, headed from one to another.

Press the Pause key

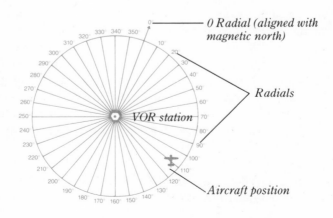

0 Radial (aligned with magnetic north)

Radials

VOR station

Aircraft position

Figure 12-1. VOR Station and Radials

45

In a sense, the OMNI knows you're there, because you're within its range. If you were not within its range, you'd have no reading on your DME. Nor would the OBI needle have shown any activity when you tuned the station. But it did. It swung way over to the right and pinned off-scale. No matter that it pinned; its reaction acknowledged your presence.

Now, if your observation of the DME told you that you're flying away from the station—away from the hub of the wheel—you read and interpreted it correctly. The DME always reads your distance in nautical miles from the VOR to which your NAV1 is tuned.

And yet, you say (if you're doing your instrument scan), the OBI reads TO. How can you be flying away from the hub when the OBI says TO?

Simply because the OMNI station, though it knows you're flying somewhere along or between its spokes, doesn't know which way the nose of your plane is pointed. It knows where you are, but not where you're headed. The OMNI doesn't know anything about headings; it deals with being. The TO is telling you not that you are flying to the station, but that from where you are now a given radial is your most direct route to the station.

Now let's find out on what FROM radial we are flying away from the VOR.

Observe your OBI (Omni-Bearing Indicator, Ol' Big Eyes) and advance the OBS (Omni Bearing Selector) headings gradually, watching for the OBI needle to get into action. Note that in the vicinity of 60 degrees it comes on scale. Stop a moment when it's centered—probably somewhere around 70 degrees (the readout you should be watching is the one at the top of the OBI).

Now, you might be inclined to believe that, because the OBI needle is centered at, say, 68 and reads TO, you are headed straight for the hub of the wheel, along spoke 68. Not true.

What the OBI is now telling you is that if you were to turn to a heading of 68 degrees and then correct to keep the needle centered as it is now, you would be on the 68-degree radial headed for the station. The OBI does not tell you in what direction you're heading or, until you set it to do so, what radial you may be on or crossing. The fact that your heading indicator (down there under the artificial horizon) says that you're heading around 200, which you are, has absolutely nothing to do with radial number 200 emanating from the VOR station. A heading of 200 is just a heading of 200; it's not a radial. You could be on any heading and on any radial, with nothing in common between them until you position your aircraft so that your heading and the radial and the OBI needle are in agreement or, in the event of significant wind, near agreement.

But we were going to find out on what radial we were flying from the station. So keep advancing the OBS. The needle soon goes as far as it can to the left, but continue to crank the selector around. Somewhere near 148 degrees, the TO disappears and is replaced by an OFF indication, which lasts through about 20 degrees while the VOR turns its thinking cap around. Then FROM appears—we must be getting warm. Persist in cranking the OBS until the needle is centered. Now you can read the FROM radial you're on or intersecting at the moment.

Notice that the reciprocal of the radial—the lower reading on the OBI— is close to the TO radial you were reading earlier. If the TO radial was 68, it's now 244, the reciprocal of which is 64. The reason for the four-degree difference is that you've been moving while you did all this. Obviously, you've moved to a new location in relation to the spokes of the wheel.

Once again, set up your OBI to center the needle with a TO indication. Now start a standard-rate turn to the left, using a 20-degree bank (and one notch of back pressure, remember, to hold your altitude), to the heading your OBI indicates. I can't tell you exactly what that is, because you're doing the flying, but it's probably somewhere in the vicinity of 60 degrees. Don't take my word for it, however; fly the heading indicated by the OBI with the needle zeroed. Remember to take off the back pressure you applied before the bank.

Once you're level, did you lose or gain any altitude in the turn? If so, use power (and power only, one notch of it) to get back to 2200 feet.

Chances are excellent that your OBI needle is not centered. Your job now is to get and keep it centered. The OBI—not the heading indicator—is your primary directional instrument from now on. If the needle isn't centered, you're not on the radial you're trying to fly. Use a little aileron, in the direction the needle is offset, to bring it back to center. Don't expect immediate results in your flying; it takes time for the airplane to turn back toward, and then fly to intersect the radial. You have to anticipate in both cases. Be conservative. Remember to correct your heading toward the needle—"fly the needle"—in all cases. When 1) the needle is centered, and 2) the OBI indicates TO, and 3) the radial you have selected and your regular heading indicator agree in principle, and 4) everything stays relatively steady, then and only then are you right on the spoke of the wheel, heading toward the hub, which is the VOR station. You'll fly right over or within a few hundred feet of it. If the OBI needle departs from center, make the necessary corrections little by little. Then wait, and make additional small corrections, until the needle is centered. Then turn immediately to the heading to which the OBI is set and see how you're doing when things settle down. The wind direction may require you to maintain a heading to the right or left of the selected radial in order to stay on it. That's what we call "crabbing," because it's akin to the way a crab crawls.

Now when you're right on, needle centered, altitude 2200, straight-and-level, and feeling very confident, wake me up.

———————————

Contact Bridgeport tower on your COM radio and get a weather check. The tower frequency is 120.9.

Let's climb to 3700 and see some blue sky. Don't use any elevator, just power, the way you learned it—two notches in Cessna, three notches in Piper. That will give you a fine 500 FPM climb.

At 3700, take off the power you put on to climb and see if your airplane holds the new altitude. If the VSI doesn't settle on zero (give it a chance to), you need more power at 3700 than you did at 2200. So use it—no trim, just a notch of power.

Keep flying. As you get close to the Norwich OMNI the OBI needle will start hopping around and then point hard right or left. The reason is that the spokes are getting closer together as you near the hub, and several radials are affecting you simultaneously. Then at 0 DME the needle pins in the direction of the actual location of the station. Watch while the OBI switches from TO to OFF at 0 DME and then to FROM. Don't chase the needle when you're close to or over the station. When you get a few miles out, it will gradually come back on scale. You'll be in the same relationship to the radial as you were before, but bearing FROM rather than TO the station.

What's happening to your altitude? Keep your aircraft at 3700 feet, not 3900 feet. Stay on top, not sixty feet under.

Now we're going to let down into the overcast again, to our earlier altitude of 2200. Give me a 500 FPM descent, and as you do, tune Boston VORTAC on 112.7. Set the course selector (the OBS) to 68, and make whatever (gentle) turns are necessary to center the needle and fly it. Don't forget back pressure before you turn, and let it off when you are level. I don't want to see any ground; I just love all this gray stuff up here.

(Piper, if you get in trouble around here, check your fuel; you can't fly on one wing—particularly if it's empty.)

By the time you level off at 2200, you should be heading about 68 degrees with the OBI set to 68 exactly, the needle centered, your elevators at operational neutral, your throttle at whatever cruise RPM will hold your altitude, your VSI on zero, and straight and level confirmed everywhere.

Meanwhile, please don't spill the coffee I'm handing you.

Have you got a match?

We're inbound for Boston's Logan Airport. Contact the control tower on 119.1. Start your let down when your DME reads ten nautical miles from the VORTAC. The station is right at the airport. Remember, use just a power reduction to enter your 500 FPM descent—two notches in Cessna, four notches if you're flying Piper.

Logan should be directly ahead of you when you get below the overcast. When your altimeter reads 1000 feet, transition to straight and level slow-flight. You know how to do that from a climb, but not from a descent, so let's learn:

Cessna, reduce your power another two notches, to 1505 RPM, and apply—two at a time—six quick notches of up elevator.

Piper, reduce your power another three notches, and apply—one by one—four notches of up elevator.

You've made the transition to slowflight.

Our runway at Logan is 22 Right. Because Piper is low on fuel, we're approved for a right turn to the crosswind leg, which heads 130 degrees. Make this turn shortly after you cross the highway, which is Interstate 93. Take a look out the left side and get the lie of the runways, then turn left to downwind leg, 40 degrees, and make your normal pattern landing.

Goose Run

Westlake Field, Redmond, WA (Local)

**North: 21390. East: 6664. Altitude: 499. Pitch: 0. Bank: 0.
Heading: Cessna 191. Heading: Piper 189. Airspeed: 0.
Throttle: 0. Rudder: 32767. Ailerons: 32767. Flaps: 0.
Elevators: 32767. Time: 8:00. Season: 3. Clouds: 0.
Surface Wind: 3 kn., 185 deg.**

Make sure your heading indicator reads 190 degrees. If not, press the Recall key.

If you have flown with me in my earlier books, you know I like to design and construct airports in unlikely places—like the one on Vancouver Island, Canada, surrounded by the Strait of Juan de Fuca, or the airstrip set in downtown New York in the shadow of the Manhattan Bridge. Awesome.

I don't just dash these off. The airport you're sitting on took me about four hours of intense cutting and trying before I made a single flight from it.

To be viable, a flying field (that's what I prefer to call these improvisations) must look like a place where you can reasonably take off and land. It has to be identifiable from the air and on radar. It can't be six miles long, because that encourages sloppy final approaches. It needs some environmental characteristics to distinguish it from an ordinary grass or pavement. It should be in an area where flying is rewarding, and esthetically pleasing.

That said, I present for your consideration: Westlake Field, Redmond, Washington.

First of all, this field is beautifully situated on the west shore of Lake Sammamish, which is why I call it Westlake Field. If you take a left front view out your window, you'll see famous Mt. Rainier across the water. You can get an idea of the size of the mountain when you realize that it is about 60 miles away. That snowcapped peak is nearly three miles high, which is higher than your "service ceiling"—the maximum altitude at which the aircraft is designed to perform reliably.

Looking 90 degrees to the left, you'll see that you're right at the water's edge, and a left rear view shows you two other mountains, Mt. Stuart (9470 feet) and Mt. Daniel (7986 feet).

Directly to the rear, you'll see how the threshold of the landing strip here at Westlake is clearly defined. Your touchdown point is just this side of where the bright green grass ends. In Cessna the landing area is dark green; in Piper it is black. And in both cases the left edge of what you can regard as Runway 19 is delineated by the shore of Lake Sammamish.

Go into radar now, and zoom to the altitude which just shows, at the very top of your screen, the shoreline taking an abrupt turn to the left. Notice how straight the "strip" you are on is, bearing exactly 190 degrees. Westlake Field is defined by the edge of the bright area behind you and the point at which the shore bends sharply left ahead of you.

Now zoom two notches higher up. You'll see all of Lake Sammamish, shaped like a galloping goose trying to take off. Notice that a highway — State 520 — points in the general direction of your touchdown point. Zoom out another notch. The highway ahead of you at the south end of the lake is Interstate 90. Both 520 and I-90 join with north/south Interstate 405. Highway 520 continues and crosses Lake Washington as Evergreen Point Floating Bridge, and then connects with Interstate 5 (a little stretch of it is visible), which runs right through the center of Seattle.

Zoom out one more notch. You can still see the abstract goose. And now you see all of Lake Washington and a long stretch of I-5. Note also that I-90, ahead of you, touches down on Mercer Island and continues to the edge of the Seattle metropolitan area, stopping short of I-5.

The water on the right side of your screen, beyond Lake Washington, is Puget Sound. Zoom out another notch to see more of it. You'll also see white spots, which represent two major area airports. The nearer one, at about one o'clock, is Boeing Field International, also known as King County Airport. The one close to the shore of Puget Sound is Seattle/Tacoma International. And the forked tributary well to the right on your screen is Hood Canal.

It's time now to see what Westlake looks like from the air. Get ready for your takeoff. We'll overfly the area this first time and get the feel of the geography. Since the field elevation is 499 feet, we'll fly at a pattern altitude of 1500. But we'll extend the normal pattern to see the sights.

Take off. Don't forget to dump your flaps and back off your power to 2105 RPM in Cessna and 2250 RPM in Piper as you climb out. But except for canceling the up elevator you used to rotate, don't trim down. We'll soon be transitioning to slowflight.

Climb straight ahead on your upwind (takeoff) heading, reducing your power to 1905 RPM in Cessna and 1950 RPM in Piper as you pass through 1000 feet. Take a look behind you at the strip you left, that sharp little area on the edge of the water, just this side of the thin patch of bright green.

At about 1400, reduce your power to 1505 RPM in Cessna and 1200 RPM in Piper and trim for slowflight. Meanwhile, what's that highway you crossed as you climbed? And what's that one ahead of you, streaking along the water?

Press the Pause key

Press the Pause key

Look 90 degrees to the right. Isn't that beautiful? I-90 zipping across Lake Washington, crossing Mercer Island on the way. On the far shore, I-5 travels south with you. And there is lots of placid water everywhere.

Directly out front, a runway has been taking shape. It's Renton Municipal, at the southern tip of Lake Washington. I-405 along that stretch is called Renton Freeway and goes straight through the city.

When the loop of lake this side of Renton Municipal is about in the middle of your screen, make a standard-rate left turn to a heading of 100 degrees (use your regular notch of back pressure to avoid losing altitude, then take it off when you level the wings).

Go into radar and zoom around until you can see the runway at Renton clearly, complete with centerline. (In Piper it will be way over in the right-hand corner.) Then press the Pause key and study the display.

Knowledge of the major highways and other landmarks in an area is more than just useful, it's indispensable. When you're flying contact—using landmarks rather than radio and other aids for navigating—familiarity with an area can point you where you want to go, or help you orient yourself if you're lost.

As you know, runways in the simulator become visible only at the last moment, particularly if they are not part of a major airport. If you're sightseeing over a sizable piece of geography, it is easy to lose track of your position in relation to the airport you left (and want to get back to) and even of the general direction in which it lies. But if you know the area, in the sense of recognizing major landmarks and how they're aligned, you can fly the way we're trying to learn to fly—with precision and confidence and, ultimately, with real expertise.

Reflect then, as you study this radar display, that Runway 15/33 at Renton Municipal points at the southern tip of Lake Washington. Mercer Island (whether or not you can see it on the display at the moment) lies in the center of the southern half of Lake Washington. Interstate 405, the Renton Freeway, skirts the eastern shore of Lake Washington and connects with I-90, which runs east and west and traverses the southern end of Lake Sammamish before it crosses Lake Washington via Mercer Island and enters Seattle. Try to "see" this kind of information and to think it while you're flying. Talk to yourself if that helps.

Press the Pause key to resume flying and get out of radar. Take a look 90 degrees to your left. There you see I-90 at this end of Sammamish, and at the far side of Sammamish, on the west side of the lake, is the little patch of green that marks the threshold of Runway 19 at Westlake Field.

Shortly you'll see another airport to your left, just across the highway at the eastern tip of the lake. That's Issaquah. When it's under your wing, turn left heading 10 degrees. As you level off, take a look 45 degrees to the left. Can you spot Westlake? If you can't, keep trying, switching to a 90-degree left view as you fly along. Keep looking left. But don't forget to do your instrument scan. Does your airspeed look right for slowflight? Are you straight and level? Is your altitude 1500? Is your heading where you want it?

When the northern extremity of Lake Sammamish (remember you're heading in the north quadrant) is about in the center of your left window, turn left again, this time to a heading of 280.

Take a look on radar and get the whole of Lake Sammamish on the display. Can you see Westlake now, just beyond the bright notch of grass, that little straight strip right along the goose's back?

Take a look out the left front of the aircraft. Can you see Westlake? Remember that the little strip of State Highway 520 almost points to it.

Switch to a 90-degree view out the left side, and watch the bright green patch come into position, telling you where the threshold is. You're flying an extended base leg. Using your best judgment, turn left to put yourself on a long final for 19. Put on carb heat and a notch of flaps, and get lined up for the threshold, just beyond the bright green and pointed right along the edge of the water.

Go through the rest of your approach and landing procedures to suit your configuration. Don't touch down before you cross the threshold. Use power to drag it in if you have to, and don't get too close to the water—but just close enough.

When you stop, take a look to your left and see how your relationship to the water compares to that of your original takeoff position. Press the Recall key when you're ready, and see the relationship exactly.

Now, if you feel like it, fly a few standard (non-extended) patterns here at Westlake. I'll get out of the airplane first, because I have a call to make. You see, what I didn't tell you about my motivation in creating Westlake Field is that this airport is virtually in the backyard of Microsoft Corporation and Microsoft Press. They are right here in Redmond, just a short distance from where we're sitting. Though I live in Florida, better than 3400 miles away, I can land here anytime I want, visit Microsoft, and say hello to my editors.

Press the Recall key

The Lone
OMNI-Ranger

Fairchild Int'l, Port Angeles, WA to Olympia, WA

North: 21739. East: 6377. Altitude: 289. Pitch: 0. Bank: 0. Heading: 265. Airspeed: 0. Throttle: 0. Rudder: 32767. Ailerons: 32767. Flaps: 0. Elevators: 32767. Time: 14:30. Season: 3. Cloud Layer 1: 7000, 4000. Wind Level 1: 4 kn., 90 deg. Surface Wind: 4 kn., 255 deg.

This weather's no surprise. Port Angeles is one of the world's wetter places. It once held the U.S. record for a year's rainfall.

Get out your Seattle chart, so we can explore our location. I want to show you some more things about tuning and understanding VOR (Very-high-frequency Omnidirectional Range) transmitters, or OMNIs for short.

Note that Fairchild International is rather isolated out here on the Olympic Peninsula; it's actually on a little finger of land called Ediz Hook, which you can see on most maps of Washington, although it isn't delineated on your chart or on radar. There's daily ferry service between here and Victoria on Vancouver Island, British Columbia.

Look at the VOR stations depicted on your chart: Tatoosh and Hoquiam on the Pacific, Bayview in the extreme north of the state (about 35 miles from the Canadian border), and then a string of four in the Puget Sound area: Paine, Seattle, McChord (Piper chart only, though the station exists for Cessna as well), and Olympia.

See if you can raise Olympia on your NAV. Then tune Tatoosh and see if you're within range of its transmitter. If you are, first use a straightedge from the airport to the OMNI center and estimate what TO radial you're on, then use your OBS to see how close you came.

How about Hoquiam? Do you think you can get a reading? Try it.

How about that? Sitting here on the ground, you're in touch with a pinpoint 75 miles away, across mountains some of which reach nearly 8000 feet into the overcast. That's hard to believe, especially since OMNI is a line-of-sight system.

Just to make sure you understand your OMNI procedure, use your OBS to get a heading to Hoquiam, as if you were going to fly straight to the VOR station. What heading did you come up with?

Now lay your straightedge on the chart so it intersects both Fairchild and Hoquiam. Get the idea?

Well, we want to fly to Olympia Airport this afternoon, so let's get to it.

There are two ways we could fly there, but contact isn't one of them, because there are no landmarks of any kind for quite a few miles. The first way to go is to find a VOR station near Olympia, which is in range, and fly toward it until we can pick up the Olympia transmission, then turn and fly inbound on one of its radials. The second way is to eyeball or straightedge a heading to Olympia using our chart, then fly that heading until we can get a more precise one on our OBI. The more direct method in this case is the second.

So use your straightedge and decide what heading you'll want to start out on. Then ready your airplane for takeoff and let's go.

Steer to keep the end of the runway straight ahead of you. Back pressure at 80 KIAS . . . take it off when you're climbing . . . get your flaps off . . . get rid of your takeoff trim . . . reduce your power for a 500-FPM climb (2105 RPM in Cessna and 2250 RPM in Piper). You're going to have this down pat pretty soon!

Turn to the heading you chose as you pass through 1000 feet. That way you'll steer clear of the Tri-motors and Spads and all. By the way, a good general rule for turning to a new heading is: Turn left for a lower number, right for a higher number, which is certainly logical enough—unless your heading is in the north quadrant. Then you have to visualize the compass rose and use some logic. If you were heading 10 degrees, for example, and wanted to head 300, you wouldn't turn right just because 300 is a higher number. But the general rule works for the majority of small turns and heading corrections.

Our cruising altitude will be 7500 feet. So climb right on up into and through the overcast. You'll need more power as you gain altitude to keep your climb rate at 500 FPM. So use it. Remember that a faster climb won't get you to Olympia faster, even though it will get you on top faster. Notice that your airspeed stays nice and fat when you hold 500 FPM.

When you're in the overcast, pin down the precise radial you want to fly, and center the needle.

What's the matter? Things aren't right? Is your heading way off what you thought? If it is, can you figure out why? Use your full scan. Is everything where it's supposed to be? Did you forget something?

This is no time to panic. It is time to think. (Of course, if everything is as you expected it to be—your estimated heading and the present radial agree within a few degrees, and you're ticking off the miles to Olympia as you tick off the altitude to 7500—then you can relax for a minute and have a cup of coffee. But if not, no coffee for you yet.)

Is everything okay on your panel? Airspeed good? Attitude right? Altimeter showing climb too? VSI confirms it? 500 feet Up? Heading? Heading what? Does that look right? Bank and turn okay?

So how about the rest of the panel? Fuel and oil okay? COM radio—haven't used it. NAV1 where it should be? Tuned to Olympia?

Aha! If your NAV1 is still tuned to Hoquiam, that's your problem. I deliberately neglected to tell you to tune your NAV back to Olympia before we took off. If you did, then kudos to you. If you didn't, then do it now. I could tell you everything every time we fly, but the more we fly together, the less I will tell you, because I won't always be flying with you.

Now, so that we'll all be flying together—as Bruce Artwick describes us, "in formation, I assume"—let's all get on the 138-degree radial to Olympia. If you're there already, fine. Otherwise, and for future reference if you don't need it now, here's how to change easily from one radial to another:

- Be sure you are tuned to the OMNI station to which you want to fly.
- Use your OBS to find out what radial TO that station you're presently on. When the needle is centered, the OBI reads out the radial you're on, but that's all it tells you.
- Turn to the heading indicated by the OBI, and point your aircraft to center the needle, flying the needle in the usual manner. You're now bearing TO the station, with your heading and the OBI course selector in agreement (though not on the radial you wish to fly.)
- Reset the course selector to the desired radial. (If it is not a viable TO radial, the OBI will read OFF or FROM, in which case set the OBI to the reciprocal heading indicated and fly that or choose a new heading.)
- Turn to intercept the desired radial, then fly the needle.

But which way and how far do you turn?

If the OBI needle is onscale, of course, you simply fly it as always. If it's offscale, here's where our wheel analogy comes in handy. If you imagine yourself on a spoke of a wheel whose spokes are numbered clockwise, you'll be able to visualize which way to turn. If you're on, say, spoke 90, and you want to be on spoke 40, you simply turn right to get over there and intercept it. If you're on spoke 120 and you want 128, you turn left.

Is a radial of a lower number always to your right, and one of a higher number always to the left? No. Because we're dealing with a 360-degree circle, remember. If you're on the 30-degree radial and want the 330-degree radial, you'll find it to your right. Think of yourself, again, as out there on the

30th spoke, looking toward the hub. Where's the 0 spoke in relation to you? And where's the 330? Even further right, right? If you use the wheel analogy and visualize yourself on a specific spoke, headed toward the hub, you won't turn in the wrong direction.

It's important to realize that, from any given position on the radials of a VOR station, the radials on the near semicircle are FROM radials, and those on the other are TO radials. Some theoreticians say we should think of the near-side radials simply as radials and the farside radials as headings, and if this helps you understand the situation it's fine with me. But also remember that no OMNI radial is a heading in and of itself. Simply heading 80 degrees does not put you on an OMNI heading of 80. You could fly a heading of 80 until your plane ran out of gas, yet never be anywhere near the 80th radial of the station you wanted to fly to or over. Only when you're on a heading of 80 degrees *and* your OBI is set to the frequency of the VOR you want to fly to *and* the course selector is set to the 80-degree radial *and* the OBI needle is centered *and* the OBI reads TO, are you on the 80-degree radial to the station you've tuned.

Now to the second part of the question above: How far should you turn to intercept a desired radial, if you've done everything else right?

The answer depends on how far you are from the station, and how big a course correction you're making. As with any wheel, the further out you go, the greater the distance between spokes.

As a general rule, if you're 30 or more miles out, turn to a heading 60 degrees higher (right turn) or lower (left turn) than your original TO heading, and fly until you intercept the desired new radial. Closer to the station, reduce the heading change accordingly, adding or subtracting 50, 40, or 30 degrees.

We are talking here about distinct heading changes, not corrections for drift, or corrections to center the needle. The general guide for minor corrections is a 30-degree cut maximum, and when you're close to the station or flying an ILS approach, corrections of only a few degrees.

Remember that you can use your other OBI, NAV2, as a check on your position throughout the change. Just set it to tell you what radial you're on, and keep centering the needle as you progress from that one to the next, and so on, until you're where you want to be.

Now, when you're on the 138-degree radial to Olympia, don't change anything. Just go on to the next flight.

Moving Right Along

Continuation to Olympia, WA

There are no parameters to set. Pick up right where you left off in the preceding chapter.

Hopefully, you're now on the 138 radial to the Olympia VOR—and because the OMNI station is right there—to Olympia Airport. You're on top (of the clouds), straight and level at 7500 feet, and it took some adjustment of your controls to get here.

In both Cessna and Piper, as your altitude increased, you needed regular advances of power setting to hold the 500-FPM climb rate. In Piper, you had to give a notch of up elevator eventually, because even full power wouldn't hold you at 500 FPM. Cessna had a notch of power in reserve.

If you applied your best procedure to the climb and to getting straight and level, your tach in Cessna now reads 2305 RPM, and you are flying with a notch of down elevator. In Piper, your elevators are at operational neutral (you took off the notch of up after you got to altitude), and you're alternating between 2250 and 2350 RPM to average out your altitude at 7500.

By "best procedure," I mean that you first adjusted power to maintain your climb, and then used elevator when power wouldn't do the job. Then, in straight-and-level flight, you took off the elevator and tried to get in balance using power adjustments. If that gave you an unsatisfactory result—didn't hold the altitude well—you adjusted the elevator, and then again power to find the best combination.

At the moment in my Cessna and my Piper, I am 30 nautical miles from Olympia. If you're in that general area, fine. If not, you may want to adjust the turn instructions that I develop below.

I'm going to show you a neat trick and give you a chance to try the radial change procedure described in the first leg of this flight. We're going to move from radial 138 to radial 170.

The following is a short synopsis of the technique:

1. Be sure you're tuned to the right VOR frequency (Olympia).

2. Find out what TO radial you're on. (If everything's as it should be, you already know you're on 138.)

3. Head to center the needle on that TO radial. (Again, we'll hope it is already centered.)

4. Reset the course selector to the desired radial (in this case 170).

5. Turn to intercept the desired radial. (If you mentally picture yourself on spoke 138—your current heading—on what you know is a clockwise-numbered wheel, in which direction does spoke 170 lie?)

So enter a standard rate turn in the direction of spoke 170, rolling out on a heading different by about 60 degrees from your original 138 heading.

I trust you turned left and rolled out on an approximate heading of 78 degrees (138 minus 60 equals 78).

Now while you're crossing the spokes, heading to intercept radial 170, tune your auxiliary navigational radio, NAV2, to the same VOR, Olympia, and use your course selector (the OBS) to center the needle. The resultant NAV2 readout will tell you which radial you're on.

However, you're soon off it, because you're flying across rather than along the spokes. So adjust the NAV2 selector fairly regularly to keep track of your progress. You'll see that you are indeed flying in the right direction to intercept 170, because the radials you're crossing have ever higher numbers. You're crossing radials fairly smartly, too, because you took an approximate 60-degree cut. A significantly lower cut would have meant an inordinate amount of time to make the change.

Notice something else interesting: Of the four instruments on your panel capable of giving you directional information, only your heading indicator and your compass agree—at 78 degrees, which is your actual heading. Your two OBIs don't agree with either your actual heading or each other. As presently set up, NAV1 indicates where you want to be—the 170 radial—and NAV2 tells you where you are—on which radial—at any given moment.

When NAV2 shows you on or near the 160 radial, the NAV1 needle pops on scale, confirming that you're ten degrees or less from your destination. When the latter needle comes to the edge of the center circle, it is time to turn and intercept. Bank to your right and get on a heading of 170 degrees.

Now immediately reduce your power setting to slowflight—in Cessna 1505 RPM and in Piper 1200 RPM. Then reduce your power another two notches. Cessna, your tach will show 1255 RPM. Piper, your throttle-position indicator will be one notch from the bottom.

Now use elevator trim to keep your descent rate as close as possible to 500 FPM. Keep trimming, and don't let that rate get too far away.

Meanwhile correct your position as needed to keep the OBI needle centered, and continue your regular instrument scan.

Given good trim procedure, your aircraft will settle into a controlled 500-FPM descent at its slowflight speed—70 KIAS in Cessna, and oscillating between 80 and 100 KIAS in Piper. Each time the glide shallows, add a notch of down elevator to correct.

When you break out of the overcast, your destination airport will be directly ahead (hopefully). The runway for which you're almost lined up is Runway 17, but your landing will be on 26 due to the surface wind, which is 255 degrees at four knots. The reason you're not exactly lined up is that your bearing is to the VOR station rather than the runway threshold. But this little experiment shows how precise an approach you can make, even to a specific runway, using just your OMNI capability—the one on your panel and the one in your head. This wasn't an ILS approach, but it was nonetheless an instrument approach in bad weather without visual reference to the ground until the very end. If you could see the airport at all when you came out of the clouds—even behind you—congratulate yourself. You're getting somewhere.

Just add power to make the transition from your descent to straight and level when you're ready. Your usual slowflight RPMs should do fine: 1505 in Cessna; 1200 in Piper. The business end of Runway 26 is to your left. Pattern altitude is 1200 feet, pattern left-hand, field elevation 206 degrees, and your best bet is to go around the airport to the right, entering the downwind leg (80 degrees) on a 45-degree angle—given, of course, that you came out of the overcast on this side of the airport.

Night Must Fall

Greater Kankakee, IL to Merrill C. Meigs, IL

**North: 16846. East: 16596. Altitude: 624. Pitch: 0. Bank: 0.
Heading: 127. Airspeed: 0. Throttle: 0. Rudder: 32767.
Ailerons: 32767. Flaps: 32767. Elevators: 32767.
Time: 19:15. Season: 4. Clouds: 0.
Surface Wind: 4 kn., 335 deg.**

Welcome to Greater Kankakee Airport.

If you're flying Cessna you're lucky, because this is one of the most beautiful settings in your simulator's repertoire, featuring a 3-D FBO (Fixed Base Operations) office and some dazzling colors.

Let's get rolling right away, because this dusk turns into night at 7:30, and I want you to see the transition in the air.

Prepare for your takeoff, which will be from Runway 34. You're parked just to the right of the taxiway. Taxi ahead and a little to your left, so your heading reads about 93 degrees; then turn right until your heading reads about 116 degrees and left again following the lights to the narrow taxiway.

When you get to 34, turn directly left, get lined up, and go ahead with your takeoff roll. Take a look behind you as you climb.

Plan to level off and cruise at 3000 feet. Meanwhile, tune your NAV1 to Chicago Heights VOR on a frequency of 114.2. Then, using the techniques you've learned, get on the 350 radial of that OMNI. Set up NAV2 to monitor your progress if you like. If you do things right, you'll be on a somewhat easterly heading as you cross the spokes toward the 350. And as you get ready to turn to intercept the radial, think about your position on the wheel, remembering that you're in the north quadrant.

When night comes down, it comes down hard, doesn't it? Aren't you glad you have learned so much about instrument flight?

Keep up your instrument scan. Everything steady. If you're on the 350 TO radial to Chicago Heights, straight and level at 3000, OBI needle centered, heading in agreement with the numbers, airspeed where it ought to be, you should feel quite confident.

And there's something real smooth and comforting about the black world ahead—isn't there? As if you were a child with your head deep down in a security blanket.

See if you can raise the Meigs tower on 121.3. If not, try the Chicago Midway tower on 128.05. If you can't reach either of them, you can always sing to yourself.

About 12 miles from Chicago Heights the world starts to turn on. There are three rotating beacons ahead. Check your chart, and see if you can identify them. If you have the Piper chart or an FAA sectional, you'll be able to name all three airports. But the Cessna chart provides little information, so I'll have to tell Cessna pilots that the rightmost beacon is Lansing Municipal Airport. Anyway, you'll shortly see its runway lights, and more beacons will spring up on the horizon.

If you're confident that you're on the 350 radial, ignore the swings of the OBI needle as you approach and then pass over the station. Then you can ignore the OBI altogether. From here on, you're flying contact. The beacon at Meigs should be right out in front of you. Fly the beacon.

However, use your DME readout from the OMNI. Meigs is about 21 nautical miles from the station, so you can track your progress from here to touchdown.

Call the tower for landing instructions. They will approve a straight-in approach, I'm sure. Check your chart for field elevation. You'll want to be at pattern altitude and airspeed about three miles out.

The highway on your left, which you're following approximately, is Interstate 57, which meets I-90 and I-94 just south of Chicago. The highway farther off is Interstate 55, which connects with 90/94 just west of Meigs.

About 15 miles from touchdown you'll be able to see I-290, which becomes Eisenhower Expressway and then West Congress Parkway in midtown Chicago a few blocks south of the Sears Tower.

When the DME (behind you, remember) reads about 12 you'll be approximately nine nautical miles from Meigs. Time to put on carb heat and back off your throttle to slowflight—1505 RPM in Cessna and 1200 RPM in Piper. Trim gradually but as frequently as you need to hold as close as possible to a 500-FPM descent.

As the aircraft slows up, put on 10 degrees of flaps and continue to trim as necessary.

From here on, your inbound flight and approach is standard. Don't forget to trim down two notches to steepen your final descent, followed by an application of full flaps. Then use back pressure to reduce your angle of descent, and again to flare, followed by feeling the yoke back gradually until the moment of touchdown.

SECTION 3

Flying For Fun

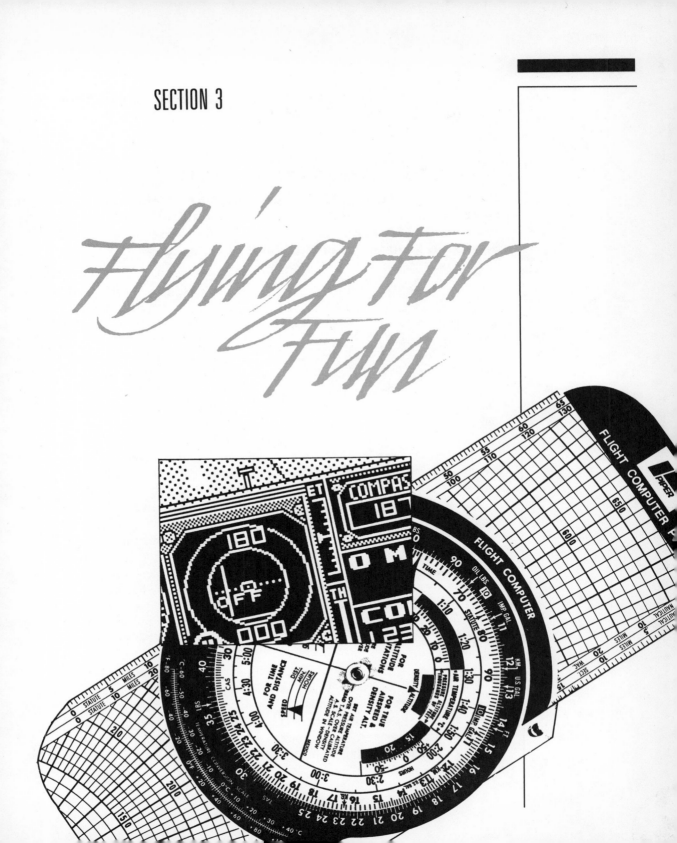

Tijuana Taxi

San Diego Int'l/Lindbergh, CA to to Oceanside Muni, CA

North: 14763. East: 6105. Altitude: 17. Pitch: 0. Bank: 0. Heading: 262. Airspeed: 0. Throttle: 0. Rudder: 32767. Ailerons: 32767. Flaps: 0. Elevators: 32767. Time: 8:00. Season: 1. Clouds: 0. Surface Wind: 6 kn., 140 deg.

San Diego has been called the only city in the country with perfect weather. Its average temperature is 70 degrees. (Just for kicks, call the tower on 134.8 and see what the temperature is this morning.) Annual rainfall is barely ten inches.

But there's more than great weather to recommend in what the San Diego Chamber of Commerce calls "America's Finest City." It has 70 miles of Pacific beaches, where you can spot giant gray whales heading south to their spawning grounds, or you are likely to find yourself swimming with a few sea lions.

San Diego's beautiful natural harbor is a port of entry for Southern California, Arizona, and New Mexico. On a hill above it, Father Junipero Serra inaugurated California's first Christian settlement in 1769. The harbor is filled with ships of every description, but particularly those of the U.S. Navy, for which San Diego is a major base. The graceful Coronado Bridge arcs high enough to let the tallest warships and other vessels pass under.

Famed WWII correspondent Ernie Pyle once described a club in San Diego called the Bottom-Scratchers. To become a member, you had to get three abalones from the ocean bottom, and also bring in a live shark by the tail, barehanded. No diving equipment was allowed, although the bottom was about 30 feet down. Prospective members carried just a flashlight, and a sharp knife for cutting the abalones loose. Only five men had ever met the requirements, and on one occasion, reported Pyle, a sea lion bit the flashlight right out of a diver's hand.

Across North San Diego Bay, which is south of where you're sitting, is the North Island U.S. Naval Air Station. A few miles west of you is Balboa Park, site of the celebrated San Diego Zoo and the world's largest collection of wild animals. Also in Balboa Park is the Prado, built for the 1915 Panama-California Exposition. Strolling through this park, you're likely to come upon jugglers, musicians, and other entertainers. And in the air around here, keep a lookout for hang gliders.

Get set for takeoff on Runway 13. It bears about 132 degrees to your left, so you'll need a sharp turn to the left to get lined up. Anyway, you should learn how best to turn your aircraft in place. The easiest way is to crank your yoke over in the direction you want to turn, then apply a notch of power; neutralize when you're pointed where you want to be.

Use radar as a directional aid if you like, and make your normal takeoff run and climb-out. Almost directly ahead of you as you climb you'll see two highways coming to a point. The one nearest you is Interstate 5, and the other one is Interstate 805. Aim for the point at which they join, in the green just beyond the edge of the San Diego metropolitan area. Level off at 1000 feet.

Now, I'm sure you've heard of Tijuana, Mexico. But have you ever been there or even flown over it? Neither have I, so let's go. It's straight ahead of us, and we'll fly over it as we cross the point at which the highways meet. And at the same moment, we'll cross over into Mexico, with the Pacific Ocean about four miles to the right. No passing through customs, and no border hassles. If you were on the ground you would have to buy Mexican car insurance, or park on the U.S. side and walk or take a cab into Tijuana. But being a privileged pilot, with your own airplane, you simply fly over all the problems.

Tijuana's fame, by the way, results from the fact that booze could be bought there in Prohibition days, and that today it has—besides alcohol—racetracks, bullfights, casinos, and other attractions.

When radar shows you're past the last short strip of highway, turn and head due west (270 degrees). You'll be flying along the Mexican border with the Pacific in front of you. The island you see is San Clemente. Keep up your instrument scan, hold your altitude close to 1000 feet, and take frequent looks out the right side. When the tip of the San Diego metro area is even with the leading edge of your wingtip (90-degree right view), turn and head north.

Tune your NAV1 to Oceanside VOR and get on an inbound radial to the station. About 30 to 32 DME miles out, you'll pass San Diego International, which will be visible out the right side.

About nine miles further north is the famous Scripps Institution of Oceanography, at the University of California/San Diego.

If you keep your OBI needle centered, you'll wind up a few miles west of Oceanside Municipal Airport, because that's how far the VOR station is from the airport. So about six miles out, transition to slowflight and look frequently out the right front. Before you get to Oceanside, you'll fly past the McClellan-Palomar Airport at Carlsbad.

Because the winds are southeasterly and Oceanside's runway headings are 60/240, you'll have to land crosswind (meaning the wind will be at approximate right angles to your heading when you're on final approach) regardless of which runway you use. So use whichever runway appeals to you. Once you have the airport in view, you need only approach and land. Elevation at Oceanside is 28 feet MSL.

ILS That Flesh Is Heir To

To Snohomish County, Everett, WA

North: 21620. East: 6737. Altitude: 2200. Pitch: 0. Bank: 0. Heading: 210. Airspeed: Cessna 114. Airspeed: Piper 122. Throttle: Cessna 20479. Throttle: Piper 21463. Rudder: 32767. Ailerons: 32767. Flaps: 0. Elevators: Cessna 32767. Elevators: Piper 36863. Time: 16:30. Season: 2. Cloud Layer 1: 4000, 900. Surface Wind: 5 kn., 155 deg.

You didn't expect this weather, but it didn't expect you either, so you're even—almost. You were sightseeing, not paying that much attention to exactly where you were flying, but you know you're somewhere north of Seattle. The first thing to do in this situation is to slow down. That'll give you more time to think, and smooth out the turbulence a bit. So get into slowflight— immediately.

Next, find out how bad the situation is. Contact the Boeing tower on 127.75 and get a weather check.

Ceiling 800 feet.

800 feet?

800 feet! Or was that 900 feet?

Either way, it's big trouble. So think. There is one ILS (Instrument Landing System)—and one only—operable in the Seattle area. It's at Paine Field, in Snohomish County, and you had better use it. This is your chance to find out if your ILS localizer and glideslope really work. If they do, and everything else comes out all right, you'll have something to tell your grandchildren about. If they don't work, or everything else doesn't come out all right, or both, then . . . well, somebody else will have something to tell your grandchildren about.

But after all, you know how to fly this airplane, thanks to your rigorous training. Here you are in slowflight. You know how to control your altitude, how to make standard rate turns, and how to climb or descend at any rate you choose, using good old power. So get to it.

You need information—all of it you can get, so tune your NAV1 to Paine VOR on 114.2. (I'm giving you the frequency because I put you here, giving you no chance to get out the right chart.) Check your DME to see how far you are from the station.

Now do everything you've learned to do. Crank your OBS around and find out what TO radial you're on, then get inbound on that radial.

Next, be advised that an ILS approach works only when you're flying a specific radial, that is, when you're on one specific spoke—the spoke that's directly in line with the runway to which you'll be guided to land. To get the correct ILS runway, and the localizer frequency you're to tune for your ILS approach, use your COM radio and tune Snohomish ATIS (Automatic Terminal Information Service) on 128.65. If the information goes by too fast, call again until you have both the ILS runway to use and the localizer frequency.

Now, using your knowledge of how to change radials, get on the correct radial for your ILS approach. And as you fly toward it, tune your NAV1 to the ILS localizer frequency—not the OMNI frequency, but the localizer frequency ATIS just gave you. After that, tune your NAV2 to Paine VOR on 114.2 to track your progress over the radials.

Now the NAV1 OBI becomes the instrument of your focus. But this time you have not one but two needles to fly—the usual CDI (Course Deviation Indicator) you keep centered when tracking to a VOR station, and a new needle, which now appears at the top of the instrument, the glideslope. The glideslope is flown like the CDI, meaning you fly toward its needle in the same way you fly toward the CDI needle. But wait until the glideslope needle gets to the center of the OBI before you start correcting. Even though you're below the glideslope now, as you get closer to Snohomish the needle will descend toward the center position.

Before it gets there, you will be rudely awakened (if you have a tendency to doze) by the signal that you're passing the Outer Marker, which is confirmed by the light under the O on your panel.

As the glideslope needle reaches the center, reduce your power setting for a 500 FPM descent. (You'll see now how valuable that descent—which you learned so long ago—is on an ILS approach.)

Now keep both the CDI and the glideslope needles centered, using just small increments of aileron for the former and throttle *only* for the latter. In this approach, you must be precise. If the CDI strays one degree, correct it— keep it centered. If the glideslope needle drifts above center, add a notch of power, or if below, subtract a notch of power to keep it centered.

Do your regular instrument scan, too, but don't be overly concerned with anything other than the OBI and its glideslope. Your VSI will reflect your power changes. You're not trying to hold 500 FPM here; that was just a starting point. What you are trying to hold is two needles, centered, precisely.

You'll see that your airspeed stays just about on your regular slowflight setting—another indication of the precision built into your flying technique.

Do not change trim. Power is your most precise tool here and will serve you well if you use it in the right amount and at the right time.

As you get closer to touchdown, stronger corrections will be required to keep the needles centered. Thus, overcontrol becomes the biggest problem. Try to anticipate the needles and stay ahead of them. If they "lean" in one direction or the other, correct immediately—aileron or power as needed.

I hope you'll be pleasantly surprised when you break out of the overcast—or at least, I hope neither of us will be unpleasantly surprised.

Go ahead and land on 16 at Snohomish. Since you've made a power-on approach, holding the aircraft in an approximate 3-degree descent angle to match the ILS, make an airliner-type approach and landing—long and flat—rather than trying to transition to your usual steeper final.

This mode is worth working on often. Here are some variations, done in the Editor, that will make it different and/or more challenging each time:

1. Change the heading parameter. Make it any number between 0 and 359 that comes into your head. Change it every time you fly the mode.

2. Change your altitude by several hundred feet, up or down.

3. Change your North and/or East parameters, adding or subtracting 10 or 15 to or from the original numbers.

4. Do any combination or all of the above, starting anywhere.

If your new altitude or position puts you too close to Snohomish, or on the other side of the airport, or too low or high, fly away from or back to and beyond the airport, or gain or lose some altitude to get into a better position.

And finally, to put a real edge on the challenge, lower the ceiling a hundred or so feet. (Before you do that, however, you'll have to excuse me. I have an appointment.)

On a Roll

Republic Airport, Farmingdale, L.I., NY (Local)

North: 17083. East: 21178. Altitude: 5000.
Pitch: 0. Bank: 0. Heading: 10.
Airspeed: Cessna 124. Airspeed: Piper 126.
Throttle: Cessna 23543. Throttle: Piper 27607.
Rudder: 32767. Ailerons: 32767. Flaps: 0.
Elevators: Cessna 32767. Elevators: Piper 36863.
Time: 14:30. Season: 3. Clouds: 0.
Wind Level 1: 5 kn., 0 deg. Surface Wind: 5 kn., 0 deg.

You're straight and level at 5000 feet, headed out over Long Island Sound. The notch of water ahead is Huntington Bay, and to the left of it is Oyster Bay, where President Teddy Roosevelt had a "Summer White House" and where his grave is. If you look straight down, you'll probably see one or both of Republic's runways.

You're here to learn how to do an aileron roll from straight and level, so let's get to it:

Cessna, give two quick notches of up elevator, followed by full right aileron. When the horizon is nearly vertical, apply full down elevator and hold it while you turn over on your back. Let the roll continue until the horizon is almost vertical again, then quickly return your elevator to approximate neutral. When the wings are about to become level, neutralize your ailerons.

Piper, add one notch of throttle, followed by full right aileron. When the horizon is nearly vertical, give four quick notches of down elevator and hold it while you turn over on your back. Let the roll continue until the horizon is nearly vertical again, then give four quick notches of up elevator. When the wings are coming level, neutralize your ailerons and take off the notch of power you added at the outset.

Note: Cessna rolls beautifully in this example and others to come. Piper (at least the Commodore 64 version), I'm sorry to say, rolls inconsistently, convulsively, and violently. I confess I have never been able to roll it with relative smoothness more than once in ten tries, and believe me I have tried—in many configurations and at many speeds—to the point where I want to crash it and let it stay crashed. The technique suggested in the aerobatic section of the flight manual simply doesn't work—at least not for me. Further, I can't conceive a roll that involves no forward pressure on the yoke at any time, but none is mentioned in the manual.

Perhaps you're flying Piper and have developed a good roll technique. If so, let me know how you did it, because I'd love to pass it on. Until then, I'll attribute the problem to the inability of the Piper computers to process information fast enough. Indeed, in mid-roll, I've seen my Piper get completely confused as to what graphic it was supposed to be displaying. And the aileron reaches the "full" position so slowly that the wing is almost vertical before you can get your elevators in the right position to hold your altitude in the roll—not to mention getting the elevators back up to neutral before you go into a dive, sickeningly, like in the old movies.

All that said, Piper, I must use the next chapter to show Cessna pilots the beautiful rolls they can do in their aircraft. I think you'll agree that it wouldn't be fair to deprive them of these. That would be like penalizing them because they happen to have higher-performance machines. And don't forget that if you switch to Cessna someday, you'll be glad to have had this special information.

So Piper pilots, use this time for practicing half rolls, which require centering your ailerons just as you become inverted and flying along upside down until you feel like rolling out again. You can do that using the present mode. Remember that your elevator control will seem to act in reverse, though it's really your perception that's reversed. To see more sky, give some down elevator. To see more earth, use some up elevator. You can also read the next chapter for some other tips, even though it is Cessna-specific.

And Cessna, come along with me. I have some things to show you.

A Cessna Roller Derby

Republic Airport, Farmingdale, L.I., NY (Local)

*NOTE: Use the parameters for "On a Roll," on page 69, except change Altitude to 82,
Heading to 80 and both Airspeed and Throttle to 0. We'll start this show on the ground.*

Runway 10 is in front of you. And so are some new thrills. Wait until you see what your airplane can do!

We'll start with a slow roll on climb-out, a little more than 100 feet above the deck. This is how we do it:

Make your normal takeoff—10 degrees of flaps and trimmed up two notches; rotate with one notch up at 80 KIAS, then one notch down when you're airborne; dump your flaps as usual when climbing 500 FPM. Then, when you're climbing at 1000 FPM:

1. Give two quick notches of up elevator.

2. Apply full aileron in the direction you want to roll.

3. When the horizon is near vertical, apply full down elevator.

4. When the horizon is near vertical again, neutralize elevator.

5. Center the ailerons as your wings come level. Continue your climb-out, reducing RPM to 2105 and fine-tuning your elevators for 500 FPM up.

How do you like that?

If you didn't get it right the first time, don't worry. That's the beauty of flying a simulator. Before long, you'll get the hang of it. And it's beautiful to do—well worth the practice.

Here are a few tips: Use your first three fingers for aileron and elevator control—the first and third for ailerons, and the one between for elevator. Hold the aileron where you put it by keeping your finger on the key; it's also a position reference. In Step 3, keep your elevator finger on the key until the elevator indicator bottoms, which happens pretty fast. But to neutralize, use a burst of quick notches up rather than steady pressure. The latter can cause you to pass neutral before you realize it, which, in turn, can pitch the nose up and cause the wing to stall. (Note that in an airplane it's the wing, not the engine, that "stalls.")

If you're in an unnatural configuration when you come out of the roll, simply use your regular procedures to correct. If you perform the roll on takeoff well, you'll still see some of Runway 10 ahead of you.

Now, while you're climbing 500 FPM with your throttle set for 2105 RPM, do another roll. Execute it just as you did the prior one. Nice, hmmm?

Next, at about 1500 feet, reduce your power to 1905 RPM and get straight and level. Then take a straight back view and, holding that view, roll again the same way, using the same horizon references as control cues.

Does this airplane roll, or does this airplane roll? And how much more satisfying to do it knowing your own coordination and skills are making it happen, unlike those toy simulators which roll over and over simply by holding the aileron key down.

Over and over, I said, hmmm? Well, let's try that. Note your altitude before you start, then:

Follow the roll procedure described above through the first roll, but don't neutralize your aileron; hold it in whatever direction you're rolling. Do, however, use all the elevator control as for a single roll. The aircraft will continue past level and enter another roll (don't use two quick ups this time). Give the same full down elevator at the same position as for the first roll, and come back to neutral elevator as you roll out of Roll Two, neutralizing your aileron as the wings are about to come level.

(If you intend to try to roll twice simply by holding the first roll through a second one, please let me out of the airplane before you start either of them. Thank you.)

While we've been doing this, Piper has been practicing inverted flights, by rolling halfway and neutralizing. So now let's do that. Just go halfway through the roll you already (if you've practiced) know how to do, and neutralize your aileron—not your elevator—as you're about to become inverted. Then begin to bring your elevators up—but not too fast—to about the quarter position, depending on your relationship to the horizon.

When flying upside down, your controls seem to act in reverse, though actually they don't. It's your perception that's reversed. Because the sky is now below the horizon and the earth above it, to see more sky apply some down elevator, and to see more earth apply some up elevator. Try to get in balance—sort of upside down straight and level—and stay that way for a bit. Remember that your ailerons, too, will seem to act in reverse. When your instincts, unreliable as usual, tell you that you need right aileron, you need left aileron, and vice versa.

Eventually, if not now, a beautiful silence will descend. Your engine will quit, and it won't start again until you do another half roll, in either direction, to get the gas feeding from the wings again. That's the gravity of the situation. (This doesn't happen to Piper, by the way, because low-wing aircraft obviously can't depend on gravity for metering gas from the fuel tanks.)

Fuel starvation limits the amount of time you can lie on your back, but it's really nice while you are doing it, isn't it?

Do a half roll a few more times, and while you're inverted take views out various windows to see how different everything looks.

Now I have another challenge for you: Set up a 90-degree view out either side of the airplane. Then do a roll, using just your artificial horizon as a guide. You'll still have a horizon outside the airplane, but it isn't the right horizon, and you had better ignore it.

One more roll, and then we'll rejoin Piper. For this one, get into slow-flight configuration. As I hope you know by now, slowflight from straight and level requires you to reduce power to 1505 RPM, then to apply six notches of up elevator in groups of two (two quick notches up—pause—then two more—pause again—and finally two more).

Let your airspeed settle down to about 70 KIAS, then be sure your altimeter registers at least 1500 feet. You will lose about 700 feet of altitude in this next roll.

The procedure to follow is almost the same as for the other rolls. The differences are that you'll use no up elevator before entering it and, when you neutralize, you'll return the elevator to its approximate slowflight position, which is about a notch and a quarter (on the elevator indicator) above operational neutral. Then, when you settle down you'll trim for straight and level and 70 KIAS.

Roll around to your heart's content now. Then we'll get Piper back in the picture and—we'll be off to sample the Scenery Disks.

The Vegas Notion

McCarran Int'l, Las Vegas, NV to St. George, St. George, UT

Scenery Disk 3.
North: 15883. East: 7230. Altitude: 2175. Pitch: 0. Bank: 0.
Heading: 340. Airspeed: 0. Throttle: 0. Rudder: 32767.
Ailerons: 32767. Flaps: 0. Elevators: 32767.
Time: 7:00. Season: 3. Surface Wind: 5 kn., 20 deg.

So you'll know where you are now in relation to the Strip and the rest of the area, go into radar and zoom until you see Interstate 15 off to your left, all of Las Vegas in front of you, and the pointed tip of Lake Mead to the east. The smaller metropolitan area to the south is Boulder City, Nevada.

The Las Vegas Strip is along Las Vegas Boulevard, which is halfway between you and I-15 and parallels I-15 into the center of the city. The section called the Strip begins with the Hacienda Hotel, just about opposite where we're sitting, and stretches north for about four miles. After the Hacienda come the Tropicana, the Flamingo Hilton (which was opened as The Flamingo by gangster Bugsy Siegel in the forties and was a flop), the MGM Grand, The Dunes, Caesar's Palace, The Sands, the Desert Inn, and a slew of others, The Sahara being the northernmost.

Howard Hughes lived in Las Vegas from 1966 to 1970. Soon after he arrived, while he was staying at the Desert Inn, he was told that he'd have to leave to make room for some bigtime gamblers who were coming to town. In response Howard Hughes bought the hotel, from a Mafia-connected syndicate, and subsequently went on a casino-buying binge.

We're going to have a nice leisurely flight this morning while I show you some sights.

That's Runway 1 Left ahead. Go ahead with your takeoff, and climb straight out over the city, planning to level off at 3300.

When you're climbing 500 FPM, take a look out the left front window and you'll spot North Las Vegas Air Terminal on the edge of town. Looking out front again, the highway going north out of the city is the continuation of I-15.

When the metropolitan area disappears under you, turn right heading 95 degrees. Do whatever you have to do to hold your altitude at about 3300.

Giant Lake Mead, which is taking shape ahead of you, is the heart of the Lake Mead National Recreation Area, which reaches all the way over into Arizona. Lake Mead has 550 miles of shoreline and is nearly 600 feet deep.

The western tip of the lake, toward which we're pointed, is called Las Vegas Bay. If you look out the right front window you may spot an airport,

Boulder City, with a section of lake pointing toward it. Switch to a forward view again and turn right heading about 120 degrees, with the idea of following the lakeshore ahead of you. Look on radar and you'll see that you're flying toward an irregular pentagon of water, with one side missing. Fly parallel to the lake, always keeping the shoreline visible to your right. Make radar checks on your progress, and stay as parallel to the shoreline as you can.

When you make the turn that puts you on a heading about 40 to 45 degrees, with further reaches of the lake visible, look straight down.

Approximately, my friend—just approximately—you're over the famous Hoover Dam, one of the world's largest. Wouldn't it be fantastic to see it down there? It's 660 feet thick at the base and nearly a quarter of a mile long, with its spillway elevation nearly a quarter of a mile high. Dam!

If the hands of your watch seem to have the jitters here, don't be alarmed. We're flying across the time boundary between Pacific and Mountain Standard time.

Head out over the lake again and track its narrowing course. After a bit, go into radar and adjust the display until you can see all of Lake Mead, shaped like a tree with two barren branches, and your airplane halfway up the trunk. Follow the branch that goes right and leads through Virgin Canyon.

Some clouds are just now crossing the sun, and a little overcast is on its way. Go into the Editor, set Cloud Layer 1 to Tops 6000, Bottoms 5000, and exit again to the flight.

Press the Editor key

Tracking the lake, you will eventually turn almost due north, and you'll see I-15 ahead on the horizon. At this point, you'll be aiming right along the Nevada-Arizona border. Coming into Lake Mead from your right is the Colorado River, which continues on its southerly trek below Hoover Dam, eventually emptying into the Gulf of California.

This is high country around here, and you'll need some altitude. Start a climb now to 4500 feet, and while you're climbing tune St. George VOR on a frequency of 109.8; then get on its 008 radial inbound.

St. George is a community in the southwest corner of Utah, only a few miles from the Arizona border to the south, and about 30 miles east of the Nevada border. It's known for Utah's first Mormon temple, which took the settlers eight years to build (1869-77). Mormon leader Brigham Young selected a construction site which turned out to be a bog. So to assure a solid foundation, the faithful had to cut thousands of tons of rock from a quarry 80 miles away and haul it to St. George.

You can't miss St. George Airport. It's right at the edge of the highway on this side of town. If you like, get into position for a straight-in approach, or enter on the base leg.

But don't misinterpret your altimeter reading. St. George is way up there—elevation almost 3000 feet. You may need some extra power, and maybe extra trim, too, as you slowfly your approach.

High Water

Bryce Canyon, UT to Page, AZ

Scenery Disk 3.
North: 16283. East: 8437. Altitude: 7587. Pitch: 0. Bank: 0.
Heading: 180. Airspeed: 0. Throttle: 0. Rudder: 32767.
Ailerons: 32767. Flaps: 0. Elevators: 32767.
Time: 10:00. Cloud Layer 1: 12000, 10000.
Wind Level 3: 6 kn., 90 deg. Wind Level 2: 6 kn., 90 deg.
Wind Level 1: 4 kn., 180 deg. Surface Wind: 4 kn., 180 deg.

It's a good thing the overcast is way up there, because you're already above 7500 feet and haven't even left the ground.

Get out your Las Vegas sectional, and place a straightedge so it intersects the Bryce Canyon OMNI and the northernmost tip of Lake Powell, which is the body of water depicted east and a bit south of Bryce Canyon. Remembering that the VOR needle points to magnetic north, eyeball a heading to fly from here to that little needlenose of water.

Get set and take off on Runway 21. You will need considerably more runway than usual, and don't bother rotating until you have about 100 KIAS—the aircraft won't take off until it's ready.

Climb straight out to 8000 feet; then turn to your estimated heading, and continue climbing to a cruise altitude of 9500. Again, because this is high country, you will need more than your standard climb power to hold your rate at 500 FPM. We'll be cruising just 500 feet under the overcast, so be sure to maintain your altitude or you'll be flying into clouds instead of under them.

It's not so easy to operate at this altitude, is it? If you were paying attention to your scan, you noticed that you were descending instead of climbing at some stages of your takeoff.

Take a look back at Bryce Canyon once you're on your heading.

Do whatever you have to do to maintain a 500-FPM climb until you level off at 9500 to 9600 feet. (If you had an afterburner, this would be a time to turn it on, wouldn't it?)

Go a little easy on your engine, that is, use trim to cruise with something less than full power.

Before very long, you'll be rewarded for your work, because out ahead of you (assuming you selected a heading of about 90 degrees) a scenic waterscape is taking shape. When you see it out the windshield, you'll also be able to see it on radar, using a very high-altitude view. You'll see I-15, too, many miles behind you.

Keep the tip of Lake Powell straight ahead. Things will remain quite fixed for a while as you fly. The distances are great up here. Sometimes only your clock will tell you that time is really passing and you're really moving.

Since we're going to take a scenic route, with Page Airport our ultimate destination, we might as well tune the Page OMNI now and see how far we are from there. Don't expect the DME to show any rapid changes, though; you're definitely not flying toward the station, but just along the rim.

Keep checking radar and adjusting it to include all of the water on the display. That will give you an idea of how large Lake Powell is.

You're flying toward Glen Canyon National Recreation Area—the point at which the Escalante River and the Coyote Wash empty into Lake Powell, which is itself fed by the Colorado River flowing down from far north. Keep correcting your course to keep the point, which soon appears as the sharp edge of a wedge, right off the nose of the plane.

Once you no longer see the tip, start a descent to 7000 feet (begin by taking off the up trim you used to get to this altitude), and follow the contours of the lake, which is really a river, staying midway between its banks; we'll track the water all the way from here to Page Airport.

If the water and the earth to either side look pretty close at 8000 feet, it's because they are.

Use radar to keep track of your position, and be sure you are flying over the main body of the lake toward its southernmost point, which is where Page Airport is. Your heading will change frequently. As you pass some of the wild arms that reach out to either side, be sure to look out your side windows and see the vistas.

At some point, when you're heading in the southwest quadrant, Page Airport will suddenly materialize in front of you. As you can see from your sectional, there's just one strip there, 15/33. Field elevation is 4310, so you will need to start your descent immediately. Use a pattern altitude of 5300 feet.

Decide from your weather information on which runway you'll land. Then decide how you will approach it. You may want to plan a steeper than normal descent to get into desirable configuration, or get into slowflight and extend your flaps sooner. But do what you have to do. Fly the airplane in. It's coffee time.

The Cape Caper

Quillayute State, WA to Ocean Shores, WA

Scenery Disk 4.
North: 21805. East: 6068. Altitude: 194. Pitch: 0.
Bank: 0. Heading: 200. Airspeed: 0. Throttle: 0.
Rudder: 32767. Ailerons: 32767. Flaps: 0.
Elevators: 32767. Time: 15:00. Season: 2. Clouds: 0.
Surface Wind: 6 kn., 190 deg.

The basic Flight Simulator encompasses four major geographic areas, which are, of course, New York/Boston, Chicago, Seattle, and Los Angeles.

You might expect that where the Scenery Disks overlap areas already covered by Flight Simulator, those areas would simply be duplicated. Not so. Though the original Seattle simulation includes the Pacific coast from Cape Flattery at the extreme northwestern tip to Hoquiam about 100 miles south (the Microsoft version includes the Astoria OMNI), the Scenery Disk for the Seattle area covers another 275-odd miles of coastline, terminating at Newport, Oregon. The westward reach, too, is far greater, extending all the way across Washington and into Idaho. Such extensions are to be expected, because the Scenery Disks cover the contiguous United States.

But there are some curious differences in the areas which specifically overlap. You are sitting on one. This airport, Quillayute State, does not exist in the original Seattle-area simulation. Nor does our destination airport, Ocean Shores, which is a few miles north of the Hoquiam VOR station. Meanwhile, certain other airports included in the original simulation—among them Spanaway, Shady Acres, Tacoma Narrows, and others—are missing in the Scenery Disk for the area. This saddens me, because the original Puget Sound-area simulation offered dozens of beautiful over-the-water takeoffs and landings. And the airports functioned as landmarks when flying the area. (Some other landmarks, too, like the Seattle Space Needle, are not in the current Scenery Disk presentation.)

On the other hand, it pleases me that the Scenery Disks are not simply carbon copies of the original Flight Simulator areas. I always knew there was an airport near Hoquiam, and I even flew out there one day to see if Bruce Artwick might have tucked it in and not told anyone, but there was no Ocean Shores in those days.

In an earlier book, I guided my readers on a flight from William R. Fairchild International to Cape Flattery, so we could see the northwesternmost tip of the United States. But as it turned out, the "tip" was not all that dramatic; in fact, it was completely rounded off in the simulation, so you couldn't be sure exactly where it was.

All three charts—the original charts for Flight Simulator (Cessna) and for FSII (Piper) and the Scenery Disk charts—are different in concept and in execution. The least helpful are the original Flight Simulator charts, which depict only major airports and VOR stations. They virtually invite you not to fly, because they lead you to believe that your explorations are limited to a few big airports. Yet much of the excitement, realism, and romance of the simulation is in the little airports. The original charts, neatly executed though they are, are also useless for flying contact, which in my opinion is the most interesting way to fly.

The original Piper charts are very detailed, showing all airports (at least I think they do) and all navigational aids. They are the next best thing to purchasing the actual FAA (Federal Aviation Administration) sectionals.

The Scenery Disk charts are adequate, considering the scope of the geography they cover. They are better than either of the earlier charts in that they show what metropolitan areas are simulated. You know in advance whether you're going to see some pavement at your destination or just a runway. Another point in favor of the Scenery Disks is the comprehensive information provided about runways. They lose points, however, for not showing state lines, so the pilot must do considerable studying of atlases (I work with about seven spread around me on the floor).

Finally, if I could ask for just a single additional feature in the Scenery Disk charts, it would be a depiction of mountains and mountain ranges similar to that now given cities and bodies of water. This for the simple reason that some topographical features of the U.S. are simulated and some are not, and the choice of which are does not seem to follow any particular pattern of either size or logic. Thus you can't know in advance, based on size or other significant attributes, whether the Grand Canyon, for example, is simulated or not (it isn't). You have to fly or at least slew there to find out. And often, where you don't expect to see a mountain, because it isn't a big tourist attraction or famous historic landmark, suddenly you see a mountain.

This afternoon I plan for us to fly this "new" stretch of Pacific coastline—first, to Cape Flattery to see if the depiction of the tip is more flattering than in the original simulation, and second, for the pleasure of making an overwater approach to Ocean Shores, on the edge of the ocean, which I anticipate will be delightful.

Press the Recall key

So obviously we'll fly north first, check out the tip (who knows, maybe the Cape Flattery Lighthouse is even simulated), then do a 180 and fly back down to Ocean Shores.

Runway 22 is waiting for us. And what a pleasant little runway it is—shorter and narrower than those big-city jobs and typical of thousands of runways at local airports all over the country.

Before we take off, tune your NAV to Tatoosh OMNI, 112.2, and find out what TO radial you're on. Then set your OBS to the 330 radial. What we'll do is climb out to 500 feet, then turn to intersect and fly 330. That radial should place us about four miles east of Cape Flattery. Then we can circle it before we head south again.

Our cruise altitude will be 2500 feet. Go ahead. I'm ready when you are.

As you make your right turn, what's your heading going to be? Remember, you're trying to intersect the 330 radial. Is it ahead of you, behind you, or nowhere at all out here?

If you're confused already, press Recall and let's do this thing right. In fact, even if you're not confused, press Recall, and go through this again anyway. Let's reason together, as LBJ used to say.

Sitting here close to the threshold of Runway 22, Quillayute State Airport (named for the Quillayute Indian Reservation just to the west, in the coastal town of La Push) in the county of Clallam, state of Washington, U.S.A., you know (or should by now) that you are astride the 334 radial of the Tatoosh VOR station 21 to 22 miles to the north. You want to take off and fly to intersect the 330 radial of that same VOR station. Remembering the wheel-and-spoke analogy, where does the 330 lie in relation to where you're sitting?

If you were heading inbound on the 334 radial, the 330 radial would be to your right—four spokes away—right? And, remembering what you learned when we did all this earlier, you would take about a 50-degree cut (the exact number is unimportant, as long as you understand the principle involved) toward the radial you want. So add 50 to 334 (as if you were on a 334 heading and on the 334 radial) and you get an arithmetic result of 384. Then, because there are only 360 degrees in a circle, subtract 360 from 384 to get 24, which is a reasonable heading to turn to after your takeoff to intersect the 330 radial.

Another way to arrive at the same conclusion is this: Because you are sitting on the 334 radial, the 330 radial has to be behind you. If you were turned around, say, taking off on Runway 4 instead of 22, the 330 radial would be ahead of you; you would fly right into it climbing straight out. If that's the way you thought and you weren't confused, congratulations.

So now take off, climb to 500, and execute a right turn to a heading of about 24 degrees, and see how readily you intercept the 330-degree radial. Then turn left and fly the needle and let's get on with this operation.

Remember, our cruising altitude is 2500 feet. If your takeoff procedure was by the book, all you will need is a power reduction to make the transition to straight and level.

Once at cruise, and with the OBI needle centered on the 330-degree radial, take a look on radar. Zoom to the view that shows the little tip to which we are paying so much attention in this flight. It certainly looks like a tip—for real, this time, doesn't it? Your nose should be pointed just a little east of it. The long hook of water beyond it is the strait of Juan de Fuca, and the land across the way is Vancouver Island, British Columbia.

Keep up your instrument and out-the-windshield scans. Keep the needle centered. Hold to your altitude. Take a look left at the wide Pacific, and take a look right at the northern section of Olympic National Park and the Olympic National Forest. Down there are Sitka spruce and Douglas firs towering to 150 feet, rare species of elk, and great mountains with active glaciers rising out of the mists of the rain forests.

Just as Cape Flattery comes into view—the tip itself in living color (green, of course) out in front of us like a slim finger of admonition—we are cheated again. The tip, the Cape, the lighthouse (if there was one), even the OMNI station, are all blown away by a disk access, and you could be flying anywhere at all. Now that's not fair! If they could show us the little finger of land ahead, why couldn't they let us fly to it? It would be different if it had been left out of the simulation entirely. But to put it there and then blow it away at the last minute is cheating.

Now if you check radar you will see something resembling a point there. It's better than nothing, I guess, so let's go ahead with our plan and fly around it. Use radar and left front views to keep a check on where it is and where you are. Fly out over the strait of Juan de Fuca, and then turn left following the shoreline.

Can you believe that the Tatoosh OMNI turns OFF when we're only a few miles from it? And that tip is very antsy, the way it jumps around.

Just this side of the "northwesternmost point in the United States," which I've made every effort to produce for you in all its drama and grandeur, is the Makah Indian Reservation. Some 400 years ago a Makah village in Ozette, about 10 miles down the coast, was buried in a mudslide, and at Neah Bay, about where you are now, there is a commemorative center displaying artifacts from that event.

Point the nose of your plane straight over what is left of the tip. At least there's more of it here than in the original Seattle-area simulation. Wag your wings, and maybe the keeper of Cape Flattery Lighthouse will beam a light up at you. As soon as there's nothing but the Pacific out front, turn left to a heading of 160 degrees.

By rights, Tatoosh ought to turn back on soon. And keep checking Cape Flattery behind you to see if it resumes the shape it had when we were approaching it.

Well, that disk access did it all, didn't it? The OMNI turns on again; Cape Flattery reaches out again; and control is returned to us.

Retune your NAV to Hoquiam, 117.7. You will have to fly a while before you are in range. Meanwhile, enjoy the immense blue of the Pacific. It isn't hard to believe it's really there, is it?

When Hoquiam turns on, get an inbound heading and fly the needle. Keep checking to your left, and see if you can spot the runway at Quillayute. Just below it is Teahwhit Head, then Toleak Point, then Hoh Head and the Hoh Indian Reservation. And when you are 45 to 50 miles from Hoquiam you will be passing the Quinalt Indian Reservation, which stretches for about 20 miles along the coast and roughly the same distance inland. Right under you as you get opposite the reservation is Elephant Rock, rising right out of the pounding surf.

Starting just about 20 miles from the station is a string of beach communities—Sunset Beach, Ocean Grove, Roosevelt Beach, Iron Springs, Copalis Beach, Olympic Beaches, Ocean City, Oyhut, and ultimately Ocean Shores, where we're going to set down.

Actually, Ocean Shores is itself on a cape, which creates a body of water called Grays Harbor, and at the extremity of which is a lighthouse. I'm not expecting to see the lighthouse, but I would like to see the cape detailed; it should make a most interesting scenic for our approach. Keep your fingers crossed.

About 20 miles out, go into radar, and zoom to the view that shows you Grays Harbor and the highway to Hoquiam, which is U.S. 12. Further east, it is State Highway 8. And indeed it does look as if there is a cape there, and out the windshield there seems to be a cape taking shape for sure.

This cape doesn't seem to have any particular name, so let's call it Cape Hope, because we hope there will be a cape when we get there.

The closer we get, the more it looks like we won't be cheated this time.

About 15 miles out you will spot the runway almost dead ahead. This is the end of the strip we want, too—Runway 14, since the wind is from the south quadrant. A straight-in approach is a natural.

Field elevation here is only ten feet above sea level, as defined by the blue Pacific. And that strip certainly does look beautiful—just a pretty sliver across Cape Hope. With an elegant approach like this, who needs the northwesternmost tip of nowhere?

Get into pattern configuration, and enjoy every foot of this long final.

Valley Low

Provo, UT to Salt Lake City Int'l, UT

Scenery Disk 5.
North: 17382. East: 8738. Altitude: 4491. Pitch: 0.
Bank: 0. Heading: 245. Airspeed: 0. Throttle: 0.
Rudder: 32767. Ailerons: 32767. Flaps: 0.
Elevators: 32767. Time: 8:00. Season: 1. Clouds: 0.
Surface Wind: 8 kn., 235 deg.

Runway 24 at Provo Airport is the shortest of the three wide strips. It points you for a scenic takeoff over beautiful Utah Lake, which is a sheet of ice this morning. The temperature is in the low 20s. I hope you're wearing your flight jacket.

Before you get set for takeoff, access radar, and zoom to the view that shows you all of the lake and the four mountains to your right. The highway directly off the tail of your airplane is Interstate 15, which goes north through Idaho and Montana to the edge of Alberta, British Columbia, and arcs south about the same distance to southern California. The mountains are part of the extensive Wasatch Range, the nearest one being Mount Timpanogos (Timp for short) which peaks at nearly 12,000 feet. The notch of Utah Lake to your immediate left is called Provo Bay.

When you return to your out-the-windshield view, take a look at Timp out the right rear window. Then look at the other hills directly to your right.

Now we come to something interesting. This is the first Scenery Disk area we have seen that features mountains. Depending on which simulator you're flying, your mountains will be black or green (assuming you are using a composite monitor). In the Cessna, for example, they're green—the same green as the grass.

Now mountains the same color as the usual simulator earth don't seem very much like mountains. With everything else so green, it is hard to tell where they begin and end.

But there is a solution. One of the reasons I find the simulators so fascinating is that they truly reward exploration and experimentation. And this morning, disenchanted with the prospect of having to mow all that green grass, I discovered how to define grassy mountains—at least those at which Cessna pilots are now looking—so you can differentiate them from "ordinary" earth. Try the trick on the next page.

Press the Editor key

Go into the Editor (do this even if your mountains aren't green) and set Cloud Layer 1 Tops to 15000, Bottoms to 13000. Make no other changes. Just exit the Editor.

Voila! Cessna simulator now has clearly defined mountains. The overcast darkened the earth but not the hills. Much better!

If you had black mountains originally, the effect is not so good. The overcast wiped them out entirely, wrapping the whole environment in a gray sheet. If this happened to you, go back into the Editor and change Cloud Layer 1 back to 0. Some of us will fly in weather this morning, and some of us won't. I don't want to fly this area, weather or not, if I can't see the mountains, because we're going to be flying around and between them. And I have no desire to fly into them.

For you green-mountain folks, the overcast trick is worth remembering whenever you want mountains to stand out from the rest of the landscape or, for that matter, when you just want to add some charisma to the environment. The color gray sometimes sheds a whole new light.

Before you get lined up and take off, read about our climb-out procedure for this flight. It'll be a bit different. We want only 500 feet of altitude, for an altimeter reading of 5000, and we want to slowfly the plane as soon as we have that altitude. Use your regular 10 degrees of flaps and your regular takeoff trim. Rotate as usual (the lift-off will not follow the rotation immediately, due to the field elevation). As soon as you are off the ground, subtract the notch of elevator you used for rotation, then dump your flaps when you're climbing above 500 FPM. Up to this point, your takeoff is normal.

Next, if you were going to make your standard climb-out, you would trim two quick notches down in Cessna, one down in Piper, as soon as you were climbing 1000 FPM. Then, when the VSI indicated better than 500 FPM again, you would cut back to your 500-FPM climb power.

But you'll remember that, if you were going to fly the pattern, you would omit the climb-out trim (the two quick notches down in Cessna, the one down in Piper) to facilitate getting into slowflight as soon as you had the altitude you wanted, because slowflight is distinguished by considerable up elevator and low RPM (1505 in Cessna and 1200 in Piper).

What we'll do in taking off over Utah Lake this morning is to compress all the foregoing as follows:

After your flaps are up, wait as usual until you're climbing better than 1000 FPM, then reduce your power setting for slowflight (1505 RPM in Cessna and 1200 RPM in Piper), and as your VSI starts down, put on your slowflight trim: in Cessna, two quick notches up, then two more; in Piper, three slow notches up with a slight pause between them.

You will wind up in slowflight at or near an altimeter reading of 5000 feet, which you'll need some extra power to maintain.

If you analyze this, what you have done is to add up elevator to your regular takeoff trim to get speedily into your normal slowflight configuration. Had you been straight and level, you would have reduced your power to slowflight RPM, then trimmed Cessna up six (2, 2, 2) and Piper up four (1, 1, 1, 1).

In any event, fly straight out over Utah Lake until you're at 5000 feet at approximately pattern airspeed (you'll fly a little faster at this altitude than, say, at 2000 feet, and you'll need 100 RPM more power than at lower altitudes, and maybe a notch of up elevator, too, to stay straight and level).

Now turn right to a heading of about 340 degrees (don't forget a notch of up elevator to hold your altitude in the turn). You will be flying along the eastern shore of Utah Lake. The highway is I-15, as you already know, and it's on its way to Salt Lake City.

Take a look at Timp out the right front and at Provo and the airport you left south of there.

Looking out the front again, we're aiming for the far side of the mountain occupying the rightmost portion of your screen. It's obscuring (unless you are way out over the lake) the two behind it. After you cross I-15, take a radar view which shows you all four mountains. They are named, in order, Timpanogos, Alta, Sunset Peak, and Mt. Olympus, the latter pointing at the southeastern tip of Salt Lake City.

Point your aircraft to fly around the corner of Alta. As it looms nearer, you'll need to correct your course to the left. And remember, you're only 500 feet AGL, so don't try cutting that sloping corner too close, unless you want to make the front page of tomorrow's *Salt Lake Tribune*.

Regularly check your location on radar, zooming in when practical to get a closeup of just the two mountains with which you're presently concerned.

Once you're over the edge, make a right turn into the valley formed by Alta and Sunset Peak, heading about 35 degrees—the point (check radar) where they come close to each other, forming a little slot. You're going to fly along the valley through the slot.

Don't turn too early, but for the maximum scenic effect, get fairly close to Sunset before you turn, so that you point right up the middle of the valley with the mountains equidistant on either side. One turn, rather than a series of them, is the way to go, and your heading through the slot will probably be about 75 degrees.

Enjoy the view on all sides as you make the pass-through. Depending on your relationship to the mountains, one view or the other will probably show you nothing but a mountain wall.

Using radar and direct right side views as guides, fly on the 75-degree heading until you're opposite the easternmost slope of Alta, the mountain on your right. And then turn 90 degrees to the left, heading—well, 90 degrees left of 75.

Once on your new heading, add a few notches of power to climb to 5500. Meanwhile keep a lookout to your left, and make another 90-degree turn to fly through the valley between Sunset Peak and Mt. Olympus. Don't stick blindly to the exact number. Fly up the valley.

This is the valley the airlines fly through when approaching Salt Lake City from the east. I haven't been to even a fraction of the places in person that you and I fly together in the simulator. But I've approached Salt Lake City as an airline passenger this way, and let me tell you, it is breathtaking. The mountains are extremely close and more massive by far than they seem in the simulator. I remember thinking then, when the weather was clear, how hazardous this approach would be on instruments and wondering whether even the airlines ever did it that way.

But when you get beyond Mt. Olympus and see Salt Lake City spreading out across the valley to your right, the sight is worth the effort.

It looked much different—bleak, grim, and inhospitable—when Brigham Young led the persecuted Mormon faithful here in their great western migration (1846–47), looked across the valley from the mouth of the canyon you just flew, and said "This is the place." He saw what it could become. And it became Salt Lake City.

The mountain out in front of you, by the way, is Deseret Peak, over 11,000 feet high and about 50 miles from here in another section of the Wasatch National Forest, portions of which are all over this area.

Be sure to take a look at Salt Lake City out the right front window as you come out of the valley. Then tune your NAV to the VOR which is just off the end of the runways at Salt Lake City International, and get an inbound bearing, centering your OBI needle. The frequency is on your chart.

You're probably about 17 miles out, but since you're already at pattern airspeed you might as well stay that way.

Press the Pause key

Now, to get nicely lined up for a straight-in approach to Runway 34 Left, the active, reset your OBS to the 340 radial, and get over there and fly it. If you don't have any trouble, we can declare you a graduate of OMNI school. If, however, you need a refresher course, press the Pause key and go back to study "The Lone OMNI-Ranger" on page 54.

You'll probably see another airport on your screen while you're switching radials. That has the imaginative name Salt Lake City No. 2.

Meanwhile a look out the right side should show you Salt Lake City International Airport, spread out there waiting for you—and a beautiful scene it is. Airport elevation is 4228 feet.

Once you're on the runway heading, attend to the rest of your approach procedure—carburetor heat, flaps, power reductions, trim, etc.—to suit where you want to set the airplane down, which is precisely on the far side of the threshold of Runway 34L. That is the place.

Honeybee

Salt Lake City Int'l, UT to Brigham City, UT

Scenery Disk 5.
North: 17636. East: 8720. Altitude: 4228. Pitch: 0.
Bank: 0. Heading: 315. Airspeed: 0. Throttle: 0.
Rudder: 32767. Ailerons: 32767. Flaps: 0. Elevators: 32767.
Time: 14:00. Season: 1. Cloud Layer 1: 15000, 13000.*
Surface Wind: 5 kn., 330 deg.

* *Only if your mountains are green. If they appear black, then there are no clouds.*

We couldn't be this close to Great Salt Lake without touring some of it. Go into radar, and view it on your display.

"Great" is the right adjective. This is the largest brine lake on the North American continent and, next to the Great Lakes, the largest lake in the U.S. One remarkable aspect is how shallow it is, with a maximum depth of only about 30 feet. Averaging 72 miles long and some 30 miles wide at its widest point, the lake has an area of approximately 2000 square miles. However, Great Salt Lake is rapidly increasing in size and has become a serious flood threat. Still, it's only a shadow of its ancestor, Lake Bonneville, which covered a major portion of the Great Basin in prehistoric times. You may have partaken of both on your eggs this morning, since 600 million pounds of salt are extracted from Great Salt Lake every year.

Speaking of Bonneville, the Bonneville Salt Flats of auto racing fame are about 90 miles west of where you're sitting.

Salt Lake City itself, founded in 1847 by the Mormon Community under Brigham Young, has a unique history as a part of the even more unique history of the Mormon Church. The story of Mormonism has the qualities of great drama and the mighty legends of antiquity, but it is a true story.

Joseph Smith, the founder of the church, was born in 1805 in Sharon, Vermont, and grew up on a farm in western New York State. Beginning at the age of fifteen, he had visions in which a heavenly messenger, Moroni, told him to found a church. The visions continued for seven years. In 1827, Smith claimed to have discovered a set of golden tablets, inscribed with hieroglyphs, which with the help of Moroni he translated and published as *The Book of Mormon*. The tablets held the record of a sacred history, including that of a migration from Jerusalem to the Americas, which began 600 years before Christ. The author of the history was Mormon, a prophet and warrior said to have lived in America in the fourth century A.D.

One of the Articles of Faith was that Zion, a New Jerusalem, was to be built on the American continent. Harassed and persecuted by outsiders for their polygamy, their claim to have divine authority, and other beliefs and habits, Smith and his followers moved west. They tried to settle in Ohio, then Missouri, then Illinois, but were attacked and driven out by other settlers. Founder Joseph Smith, imprisoned in Nauvoo, Illinois, for destroying the presses of a newspaper that had criticized Mormonism, was lynched by a mob. He was succeeded by Brigham Young who, hoping to find refuge from persecution for the church and its followers, led an advance party of 143 men, 3 women, 2 children, and 72 covered wagons 1400 miles across the Great Plains from Nauvoo to what came to be known as the Jordan Valley, in which Salt Lake City is situated and where he finally made his historic "This is the place" proclamation.

The advance party was followed by thousands of the faithful in wagons and on foot with their few belongings on their backs or in pushcarts. Hundreds died of exposure, disease, and starvation enroute. In Utah, which they called Deseret (which does not mean desert, but is the Jaredite word for "honeybee" in the Book of Mormon), they fought an Indian war, built systems to use melting snow from the mountains for irrigation, and gradually converted the bleak landscape into farmland. Today, the agricultural aspects of Salt Lake City have given way to residential neighborhoods, green lawns, trees, and beautiful gardens. The most notable structures in the city are the Mormon Temple in Temple Square and the great Mormon Tabernacle, famed for its construction and acoustics and for the Mormon Tabernacle Choir. I was privileged to climb up many flights of steep, narrow wooden stairs and through the mighty rafters of the Tabernacle with a Mormon business friend as my escort. There is not a single nail in that incredible timber structure. It is meticulously and lovingly fitted to endure forever, locked piece by piece, as it soars heavenward, with hand-fashioned wooden rods and spikes.

But it's time that we were on our way. Runway 32, a short strip crossing the parallel major runways at an angle, is just to your right.

Since the Great Salt Lake is 4202 feet above sea level, let's plan a cruise altitude of 5500.

As you climb out, you'll see hilly Antelope Island on the left side of your windshield. Make a standard-rate turn to the left to skirt its southern tip, starting as soon as you reach your cruise altitude. Roll out on a heading of about 230 degrees. Then when you're clear of Antelope, correct your heading by approximately 10 degrees to the right so that you are aimed toward the southern tip of the second island, which is Carrington Island. Use your radar to observe where you are going, and aim to follow the lake where it bends around Carrington. The big mountain on the left of your screen is the one we saw when we flew out of Provo—Deseret Peak.

The highway along the south shore, visible out the left side and, shortly, ahead of you, is Interstate 80, also known as the Dwight D. Eisenhower Highway, which traverses the Great Salt Lake desert. There are three major military installations out there—Hill Air Force Range north of I-80, Wendover Bombing and Gunnery Range, and Dugway Proving Grounds south of it. Further west, near Wendover and just this side of the Nevada border, are the Bonneville Salt Flats.

A left rear view during your flight toward beautiful Carrington Island reveals Timpanogos, Alta, Sunset Peak, and Mt. Olympus, punctuating the landscape between Provo and Salt Lake City.

Follow the lake clockwise around Carrington, then fly approximately parallel to the west shore.

When you're about a third of the way up the lake, look on radar and you'll see Promontory Point at about two o'clock. Take the maximum closeup view that includes the point, squared off on three sides. Turn to aim at the center of the near side. Your heading will be approximately 6 degrees, and you'll soon discern the point through your windshield.

If you look at your Salt Lake City Sectional, you'll see what's happening. You're heading in the general direction of Brigham City, Utah, and its airport. Now that you know where you are going, fly it as you see it. The one runway at Brigham City is 16/34, the same numbers from which we departed Salt Lake City International. So you know what direction to land. Use your chart to help you get into position, paying particular attention to your bearings with respect to the lake and I-15 going north out of Salt Lake City; in other words, fly contact. After all, that's why there are mountains, rivers, lakes, highways, and cities in the world—to help pilots locate airports.

An Eerie Eyrie
of Eagles

Eagle Field (Local)

**North: 17417. East: 7447. Altitude: 410.
Pitch: 0. Bank: 0. Heading: 40. Airspeed: 0. Throttle: 0.
Rudder: 32767. Ailerons: 32767. Flaps: 0. Elevators: 32767.
Time: 12:00. Season: 2. Clouds: 0. Wind: 0.**

Somebody parked the plane on the wrong side of the hangar! OK, I did it just to give you some extra taxi practice now that you're no longer a beginner.

I told you earlier that we would come back some day and explore those mystery airports that look just like Eagle Field and seem to be scattered all around the fringes of this particular simulator geography.

I have a feeling that if we took off from any runway in Red Quiver Valley and flew a beeline, we would pass five Red Quiver Valleys and then come to a sixth, which would be this one. That would be a total of seven of them in existence. But on the other hand, seven is an odd number which belies the possibility of mirror images, which these Valleys seem to suggest.

Also, if the phenomena occur regardless of the direction in which we take off, then maybe there are three Valleys in each of four directions, which means there are 12 altogether. But still, there's the so-called "home" valley, which would be a thirteenth.

I think a first reasonable step would be to fly to a relatively nearby clone Red Quiver Valley and land there, whether there's a runway or not. Then we could look around a bit.

What we'll do is take off from Runway 27, the one we flew from when we practiced pattern flying, and fly straight on the runway heading, 270 degrees, until we come to something.

So get ready for takeoff, and taxi ahead around to the far side of the hangar. Use your radar to show you the lie of the taxiway and runway. Come back to the text when you're lined up and ready for the takeoff run. You must be lined up on a heading of exactly 270, so taxi around and try again if you don't nail that heading the first time.

Before takeoff, I want to call your attention to a few things. I've selected a crystal-clear day, so there are no clouds for anything to hide behind. I've selected the most unmysterious hour: high noon. There isn't even a wind. If someone tries to play a trick on us (like, perhaps, Bruce Artwick), he will have to be pretty swift. This will be an entirely scientific expedition, so I trust you will take notes along the way.

Go ahead with a normal takeoff, except don't trim down at all after you rotate, and keep all your power on (but do dump your flaps as soon as you're climbing 500 FPM). You'll leap right over that mountain at a rate of climb you haven't seen for a while. (Piper, you may want some up elevator near the summit. It isn't necessary, but if you want it, use it.)

Right after you dump your flaps, go into radar and adjust until the whole eastern (lower) portion of the grid is displayed and you see the river ahead, then your plane, and then the airport behind you. Then press the Pause key.

Now this is important, so write it down:

You're flying due west. The river starts in the third gridbox from the eastern border and flows approximately north and south across the grid. Note that the airport, Eagle Field, is situated one mile west of the eastern border and four miles south of the northern border of the grid. Draw a picture or something, because if we find no runway and no hangar when we get where we are going, we are going to land in the box where the runway is supposed to be. So put an X there. The second north/south gridline will act as a runway threshold for us.

Now resume your flight over the mountain. And leave your ailerons completely alone. You're already supposed to be on a heading of exactly 270. For a thrill, watch the mountain go by off your left wingtip. See the white peak down there?

Once you clear the mountain, get straight and level at an altitude of 6500 feet. This requires, in Cessna, two quick notches of down elevator, plus one additional notch down to cancel your rotation back pressure; and in Piper, two slow notches down (plus whatever you may have used to clear the mountain). Both aircraft will now be at operational neutral. Then use power to get to, and hold, your cruise altitude.

Before you fly too far, look back at the stage setting we are leaving (but keep flying, don't pause). Note that the arrow on the hillside appears on this side as well as the other; it could be an important landmark. And observe that the area is bounded on the north and west by mountains, but is open on the east and south sides.

I know from experience, and perhaps you do also, that a clone of Red Quiver Valley always seems to appear simultaneously with the disappearance of the original, or of another clone. So once you're straight and level, I recommend that you fly with a permanent rear view until the area you have just left disappears. There's nothing to see out front anyway, and I assure you that out here in no-man's-land the chances of a midair collision are vanishingly low.

Press the Pause key

91

When Red Quiver Valley immaterializes, look to all sides until you see Clone 1. Then, again, return for the next segment of text.

That happened pretty fast, didn't it?

OK, Clone 1 is straight ahead! I really didn't expect this, did you? Flying in other directions we see two clones, to the left and right, before we see one straight ahead. We're in luck!

Furthermore, it looks as though we're on a perfect heading for Runway 27—and maybe there *is* a runway down there.

You had better start your descent right away, and on the way down slow the airplane so you have some time to take stock of the whole situation. Just set up a descent at about twice the usual rate and then keep trimming up and reducing power until you're descending 500 FPM at your slowflight airspeed.

Though you know where the runway is supposed to lie (X marks the spot), I suggest that you not be too hasty about changing your direction until you're close enough to be sure you have to.

Remember your carburetor heat, and put on some flaps when you think it's time for them.

I certainly don't see a runway down there—or a hangar, either. Do you? But everything else is right where it's supposed to be. What's going on here?

Keep a tight control on your aircraft. Use all your flaps if you think you need them. Change power and elevator settings as needed. Fly the thing. Make it do what you want it to do, which is land right where Runway 27 is supposed to be.

Remember the field elevation of 410 feet—at least that's what it was at Eagle. And I wouldn't mess with aileron here. Because there's obviously no runway there, if you're off a hair, just land straight ahead as close to the projected spot as possible. Whatever you do, short of landing in the river, get the airplane down on the ground.

And whatever you do, don't crash, or you'll have to fly the whole thing over again.

Now, on the ground, look out all sides. Everything is where it's supposed to be: the mountains, that is, and the gridlines. But there's no runway, and no hangar.

Look on your radar. You see the same grid, the same river, the same airplane—everything but the runway.

Now exactly what is happening here? Why has Bruce Artwick included this clone of the real stage setting we left a while ago? (And there are other, similar clones, I guarantee you.)

These are, of course, World War I zones, even though we used Eagle Field as a training field and got in there with our full panel of instruments (which you don't have when you play war).

Another question has to be asked: If the simulator has a clone or clones for this particular scene, does it have similar clones for everything in the simulator world? Are there two or seven or eleven Manhattans, Meigs Fields, and Marina del Reys?

And if the answer to that is yes, then there must be a similar number of clones for the entire U.S. on the Scenery Disks. That is impossible; there isn't room in my computer for eleven Texases.

No, the cloning must be unique to the World War I zone. And again the nagging question—why?

There is something we can do that may reveal part of the answer. That's go into the Editor and see what the North and East parameters are, right here where we're sitting (don't do it yet). Our altimeter tells us that the altitude is the same as at the original Eagle Field. But if the Editor reveals that we're actually *on* Eagle Field now, in the same spot, with just the runways and hangar somehow magically erased, we'll have a new aspect of the mystery to ponder.

My proposal is this: Go into the Editor and compare the North and East parameters of where we're sitting with those at the start of this chapter. Remember, we taxied from the original location, which was at the west end of the hangar, so there will be a slight change in numbers, but it shouldn't be all that great.

Before you go into the Editor, restore your forward view if you haven't already, and note the position of the arrow on the hillside. Now go into the Editor and find out exactly where we are.

My North position reads 17421; my East position, 7193. Your numbers will probably vary by a few digits from these. Now, the original North parameter was 17417, and East was 7447. The difference between Norths is only four digits, not even the length of a typical runway. But the difference between Easts is 254.

Two hundred fifty four is many, many runways. We are definitely not anywhere near the original Eagle Field. The slight difference in Norths is perfectly logical, because we flew due west. Except for the effects of compensation for the orthogonal coordinate grid overlaid on the Lambert Conformal Conic Projection, plus slight deviations due to the computer being shaken by engine noise, our North position might not have varied all the way.

Well sometime in the near future I'm going to do some further exploration, trying to find a third and perhaps fourth or seventh clone using the same present scientific method. I'll invite you along when I do.

Press the Editor key

Meanwhile, I have a neat idea: Let's exit the Editor now and taxi straight ahead along the ground to and across the river, to see whether it's really a river, or whether we can taxi through it as if it weren't there.

So go ahead. Exit the Editor now, and taxi forward and across the river. Get your flaps up and carb heat off, use full down elevator, and you can push the throttle to the wall without taking off.

Space Nocturne

Roswell, NM Industrial to El Paso, TX Int'l

Scenery Disk 2.
North: 13907. East: 10580. Altitude: 3671. Pitch: 0. Bank: 0.
Heading: 300. Airspeed: 0. Throttle: 0. Rudder: 32767.
Ailerons: 32767. Flaps: 0. Elevators: 32767. Time: 17:10.
Season: 1. Clouds: 0. Surface Wind: 8 kn., 290 deg.

Press the Pause key as soon as you confirm that you're lined up for Runway 30 here at Roswell. It's dusk, and in 20 minutes it will be night, and we want to save all the daylight we can for our flight to El Paso.

But first something about Roswell, New Mexico.

It's hard to believe that it was 60 years ago, in 1926, that Robert Hutchings Goddard, the great American physicist, fired the world's first liquid-fuel rocket, eventually earning a Guggenheim grant to set up a developmental station near where you're parked here in Roswell. It was a small rocket by today's standards, but Goddard's contribution to what was to become America's space program is incalculable. He developed most of the fundamental ideas behind modern rocketry, and among his more than 200 patents is one for a multistage rocket. Yet, sadly, he died in 1945 before his work was recognized by the U.S. government. By that time, German scientists under Wernher von Braun had developed the liquid-fueled V2 which carried an explosive warhead weighing a ton—the ancestor of our modern space rockets.

Curiously, the first rocket-engine flight to carry a human being was that of Fritz von Opel, the German manufacturer of the Opel automobile. Just three years after Goddard's historic rocket launch, on September 30, 1929, Opel went aloft in his own small rocket-powered craft, covering nearly two miles in a flight of 75 seconds. This is a fact largely overlooked.

Pioneer Goddard's early rockets are on display in the Roswell Museum and Art Center.

Press the Pause key

Press the Pause key again, and tune your NAV to the Piñon VOR, named for the little New Mexico town in which it is situated. Center your OBI to see what TO radial you're on at present. Then press the Pause key again.

Press the Pause key

Maybe I should mention that you could take off and then fly to get on the radial indicated by your OBS now, which is probably 206. An alternative is to reset for a more convenient radial once you're airborne, which is the procedure we'll follow this time.

If you look at your Albuquerque/El Paso sectional chart you'll see why we're using Piñon: The Newman OMNI, five or six miles north of our El Paso destination, is out of range at this distance. In such cases we use the VORs as stepping stones, particularly when we have poor visual references, as we will on this flight.

Speaking of visual references, let's get going while we still have some daylight. Take off and climb to 4500. Our cruise altitude will be 6500. But as soon as you're at 4500, re-center your OBI needle and get on the indicated radial for Piñon.

Take a look at the metro area of Roswell on your right as you climb out. Keep your climb rate as close to 500 FPM as possible.

When you reset your OBS, you'll discover that there's only a minor difference in radials. You could as easily fly to the 206 as to the—what? I'm getting on the 204 now, so I have obviously flown only two degrees from the original. Anyway, just so we'll all be in the same situation, fly the 204 radial.

As your altitude increases, don't let your rate of climb slip away. Add power as needed. And when you level off at 6500, don't be in a hurry. If you back off your power too much, you'll quickly drop below your cruise level. Easy does it, and watch your VSI and altimeter. They'll tell you what's happening if you monitor them.

Remember the alternative of elevator trim to maintain altitude, and remember that the preferred trim in such instances is one notch down, which results in better airspeed.

Before you've been at altitude very long, the bleak landscape ahead will brighten a bit as a highway comes into view. It's north/south Interstate 25, and it will probably relieve us of having to fly in absolute blackness even when night falls in a few minutes.

Besides your altitude, don't let the OBI needle get away from you. Never hesitate to correct for something you know is wrong. Sometimes a flight like this weaves a hypnotic spell, and you think your only responsibility is to sit there while the airplane flies itself. It doesn't. You have wind to contend with and a relatively difficult altitude to manage. So contend with it and manage it.

When night comes, the blackness ahead becomes velvety, doesn't it? Turn off your lights for a moment, just to see everything reduced to its maximum simplicity. With such visual austerity and its accompanying loneliness, you could be thousands of miles out in space.

Why do you have to keep correcting to the right all the time to stay on the 204 radial? Well, you have an eight-knot wind from 290 degrees, so it is hitting you just about broadside, trying to blow you over to the adjacent spoke. Once you get pointed in the right direction, though (which isn't on a heading of 204), you will be able to keep the needle centered fairly easily. You'll be crabbing—moving slightly sideways through the air with your nose pointed to the right of your actual direction.

When your DME reads five miles from Piñon, tune to Newman VOR on a frequency of 112.4, and get on a new heading inbound for that station. The "prototype" radial (the one I'm flying) is 230. But suit yourself.

As you flew by Piñon, incidentally, you were in a sort of valley between the Guadalupe and the Sacramento mountains, both part of the Lincoln National Forest.

Aren't you pretty proud of yourself and the skills you have developed? Here you are flying entirely on instruments (unless you want to call that white line a visual reference) in solid command of your airplane, knowing exactly what you're doing, where you are, and where you're going. You are truly on top of things.

About now you're over the sprawling Fort Bliss Military Reservation. Also about now, or very shortly, you'll be able to check your radar and see El Paso on I-25 (which changes numbers to I-10 going south and east out of the city, near the top of your display).

Slightly less than 50 miles out, the city will begin to be perceptible on your screen, as a break in the highway. If you like, you can use a combination of your front and radar views to take over visually from here. Head for the approximate center of the city, because that is where El Paso International is.

The city of El Paso is just inside the western tip of Texas and just this side of the Mexican border, which is delineated by the Rio Grande River. You're flying to the tiniest piece of Texas you'll ever see. Airport elevation is 3956 feet, so you won't need to start your letdown very far out.

There are three strips at El Paso International, which means there are six runways. Get out your Scenery Disk airport information and decide which runway you're going to land on.

And get plenty of sleep tonight. Tomorrow we're flying north from El Paso, and I am going to introduce you to some fancy, advanced airwork.

Long Ways Around

El Paso, TX Int'l to Las Cruces, NM Crawford

Scenery Disk 2.
North: 13423. East: 9814. Altitude: 3956. Pitch: 0. Bank: 0.
Heading: 80. Airspeed: 0. Throttle: 0. Rudder: 32767.
Ailerons: 32767. Flaps: 0. Elevators: 32767.
Time: 7:30. Season: 1. Cloud Layer 1: 20000, 18000.
Surface Wind: 4 kn., 250 deg.

Turn the airplane around so Runway 26R is ahead instead of behind you. The best way to execute a turn like this—a turn in place—is to apply ful aileron (or rudder if you're flying Reality mode) and then apply power. You can virtually turn on a dime.

Go into radar and zoom to the view that shows you all of El Paso, with I-10 going through it and the Rio Grande skirting its southern edge. They parallel one another north, and we're going to follow them to Las Cruces, New Mexico, with some interesting detours en route.

Go ahead with your takeoff. Plan on an initial cruise altitude of at least 5000 feet.

Using radar to judge where to turn, get lined up with the longest straight stretch of highway off to your right. You'll turn just about as you leave this section of the El Paso metropolitan area. Position the aircraft so you're pointed straight up the road. Your ultimate heading will be about 320 to 325. When the highway is straight ahead of you, press the Pause key for a moment.

The city ahead of you is Las Cruces, New Mexico, home of New Mexico State University. Look at that mountain at about 11 o'clock.

The first advanced maneuver you're going to try is the chandelle. Isn't that a beautiful word? It's French for "candle," though how a candle relates to the maneuver is something I haven't figured out.

The chandelle is a maximum-performance climbing turn involving a 180-degree change in direction. If it's done perfectly, you should wind up flying in the opposite direction with zero bank and with your airspeed just above stalling, while gaining the maximum possible increase in altitude. Follow the steps on the next page (but remain paused and don't try the maneuver until you have read through to the noted paragraph on page 100).

Press the Pause key

Chandelle

1. Apply full throttle.

2. Pitch the nose up (using elevator) until the horizon is just visible at the bottom of the windshield.

3. Apply and release aileron in the desired direction of turn, continuing upward elevator pressure to maintain maximum climb (minimum airspeed above stall).

4. Neutralize aileron on 25-degree bank indication, and maintain that bank.

5. Continue gradual upward elevator pressure to keep minimum amount of horizon visible without stalling aircraft.

6. Begin a slow, gradual rollout (touches of opposite aileron) halfway (90 degrees) through the turn, continuing to apply back pressure for maximum climb.

7. Level the wings when the 180-degree turn is completed.

8. Adjust elevator and power for straight and level.

You should gain well over 1000 feet by the time you have completed the chandelle—about 1500 feet can be regarded as optimum. If you gain close to 2000, your turn is too conservative.

If you get a stall warning along the way, give a notch of down elevator, then another if necessary. Don't overreact to the stall warning with too much down elevator, or you'll spoil the maneuver. Note at what airspeed you got the warning, which will help you avoid it on your next try (though the stall will occur at different speeds based on your angle of attack). Just below that airspeed is where you want to try to stay throughout the maneuver.

Also determine, as you practice the chandelle, how much elevator puts you at the maximum-performance pitch attitude at the outset. But don't start the turn until you have the desired pitch, the primary objective being not a high-speed turn, but a maximum-performance climb while turning.

Like all other precision airwork, this maneuver is a challenge. It will take some practice before you do it well. But it's a beautiful thing to do and see. (And one day, with the coming third-generation simulators, we'll be able to watch it from somewhere outside the cockpit.)

Press the Pause key

Press the Editor key

Press the Save key

Press the Recall key

Note: At this point you're ready to try the chandelle. But first you are going to enter the Editor—not to change anything, but simply to save the parameters of your present configuration for practice purposes.

So press the Pause key, go into the Editor, press the Save key specific to your computer, and exit again.

Now try the maneuver. If you don't like the way it comes out, which undoubtedly you won't the first time or maybe the fiftieth, simply press your Recall key and try it again.

When you're through practicing, press the Recall key, and you will find yourself at 5000 feet headed up what is now I-25 toward Las Cruces.

Now we'll try Eights Along a Road. The idea here is to describe a figure eight at right angles to the road we're following, while not gaining or losing any altitude, winding up on the same heading with which we started.

Eights Along a Road

1. Position yourself so the road is straight ahead of the nose of the plane.

2. Using your normal notch of up elevator to hold your altitude, enter a bank of any magnitude and fly a circle to the right. Use additional elevator as necessary to hold your altitude.

3. Try to complete this top loop of the eight just as you describe a 45-degree angle across the road.

4. As you cross the road, immediately bank left, and fly another circle in the opposite direction, describing the bottom loop of the eight.

5. As you complete this loop, roll out with the road once more straight ahead of you, and on your original heading.

This sounds easy, but like everything else, it's a difficult maneuver to perform really well. You should decrease your bank slowly as you near the end of the first circle, crossing the road in a level attitude. The second circle will end with you turning to your original heading at the now well-worn spot where it all began.

Use radar and any of your out-the-window views to keep track of your progress. And be sure that you've crossed the road before you start off in a new direction. A down view here is very helpful, because the road disappears from your front windshield view well before you've actually crossed it.

Even executed on the trailing edge of adequacy, Eights Along a Road (you can do more than one, of course) let you look over the whole geography around you pretty thoroughly, and are useful for viewing a particular scene from all angles. More important, they hone your precision.

Another maneuver, Eights Across a Road, is exactly the same, but is flown starting at a 90-degree angle to the road in question.

The ground has been gradually rising under you, so climb to 5500 somewhere along here. Then fly a couple of eights, if you like, as you progress toward Las Cruces. This might be a good time to do a couple of rolls, too, just to keep in practice. And while you're in one of them, fly inverted for a minute to see what a straight line looks like upside down.

But don't try these tricks unless you've mastered the procedures described in earlier chapters and can do them without losing altitude. You haven't any to spare here—about 500 feet maximum. In fact, you're just about at pattern altitude for Crawford Airport: elevation 4454.

Lacking trees, houses, and other vertical and three-dimensional references, you can easily be deceived about altitude in the simulator. A feeling for the various elevations of an area is almost mandatory. The best references for elevation are the FAA sectional charts. The next best is the simulator sectional chart for the area you're flying. I confess that once I was cruising along somewhere over Texas, thinking I was about 1500 feet AGL, when suddenly I heard my tires squeal—I had made a straight-and-level landing in the prairie.

Your landing at Crawford will be on Runway 26. The airport is west of the city and, for that matter, west of the river. So get over to your left and line up following the Rio Grande. You will see the airport ahead before long.

You will see another highway, too, crossing the river. It's Interstate 10, which we last saw south of El Paso, and here it crops up again.

Runway 26 nearly parallels I-10. If you stay close to the river and at the last get on a heading of 350, you'll be on a left base for 26 before you know it.

101

Apple Polishing

Manhattan Island, NY (Local)

Flight Simulator Disk.
North: 17065. East: 20996.
Altitude: 23. Pitch: 0. Bank: 0. Heading: 220. Airspeed: 0.
Throttle: 0. Rudder: 32767. Ailerons: 32767. Flaps: 0.
Elevators: 32767. Time: 5:30. Season: 3.
Cloud Layer 1: 9000, 8000. Surface Wind: 7 kn., 210 deg.

Be sure (you should always check this) that your heading agrees with the heading set up in the Editor: 220 degrees.

This is the flying field I created in Lower Manhattan—a convenient spot for us to begin a little tour of New York. I will try not to repeat myself for those of you who have flown out of here with me in the other books.

You're looking at Manhattan Bridge, which connects the boroughs of Manhattan and Brooklyn. A look out the right front window will show you the World Trade Center towers and (just a slip of a thing from here) the Statue of Liberty. Out the right rear window, you'll see the Empire State Building. These, together with Central Park and a few major avenues, comprise all the visual features of the Manhattan simulation.

The two most exciting features are the Manhattan Bridge and Lady Liberty. The bridge is so realistically digitized that its roadway will support you.

Let's have a close look at the bridge and at the same time learn a new maneuver, which we'll also use to view the Statue of Liberty. It's called Turns Around a Point.

There's an altitude discrepancy here at Manhattan Airport; your altimeter probably reads between 500 and 600 feet, but the altitude given at the beginning of the chapter, 23 feet, is the actual altitude, even in the simulator, though the simulator has trouble recognizing it. If you were to take off and then land again, the altimeter would read correctly. But something, I have no idea what, flaws the reading here until you have been flying.

Now go ahead and make your normal takeoff, but transition to slowflight once you're airborne—as if you were flying a pattern. Here is a short recap of the procedure (if you need more detail see "Flying the Pattern"):

After you dump your flaps, do not adjust elevator trim. Reduce your power to 2105 RPM in Cessna and 2250 RPM in Piper, and continue climbing. At your desired altitude, further reduce power to 1505 in Cessna and 1200 in

Piper. If flying Cessna, follow this with two quick notches of up elevator, pause, and add two more quick notches of up. In Piper, use three slow notches up with about a second between. This will, at altitudes of 2000 feet or less, get you into slowflight configuration.

This morning the power reductions outlined above will take place fast, because we want to get straight and level at about 1000 feet, so the second set of reductions — to slowflight RPM — will come shortly after the first.

You will have passed Manhattan Bridge by the time everything settles down, so at that point take another look at it out the rear.

Looking ahead again, Upper New York Bay is on your right. Where it curves to the left is known as The Narrows, through which the water wraps around the southwestern shore of Brooklyn and empties finally into the Atlantic Ocean.

Make a standard-rate turn over the bay to a heading of about 20 degrees or whatever puts both the Trade Center towers and the Empire State Building ahead of you with the aircraft pointed about midway between them.

Fly this way for a few seconds, then turn right again and point so that the Manhattan Bridge is well to the left on your windshield, and you're flying to the right of it. Take a look out the left front and then the left side, and about the time the suspension girders on the Brooklyn side disappear from view, give one notch of up elevator and bank to the left.

The idea now is to continue banking and turning so that you circle the bridge, keeping it always in view off your left wingtip. (If you were too close to sight the bridge on your first pass, use radar or out-the-window views and maneuver to get it off your left wingtip as described.)

Establish whatever relationship with the bridge suits you. You can circle, keeping just a portion of it in sight, or you can fly farther out and circle the entire bridge. The key thing, once you like the view, is to keep the bridge apparently motionless from your left side perspective. This is called Turns Around a Point, although in this case it's a pretty big point (when we do it at the statue it will be a tighter turn).

How do you keep it motionless? If the object you are viewing and circling moves toward the tail of the plane, increase your bank a bit; if it moves toward the nose, that is, it is getting ahead of you, decrease the bank a bit. If you want to get closer to the whole scene, straighten up and fly closer, then set up the turn; to get farther away, do the opposite.

Since we're turning around a long structure in this case, pick a point, such as the center of the bridge, as your reference point which you want to keep virtually motionless. Tie it visually to some area of the wing.

Isn't this an elegant way to view something? You see it and its whole environment from every perspective. And you can view it for as long as you like.

If you had trouble getting this scene and this maneuver the way you wanted it, don't concede. This is one of the most useful of all flying tricks, and the basic idea can be expanded or contracted to suit any viewing situation. For instance, expanded, it permits you to circle an airport until you have its layout firmly in mind, then decide where you want to land. Or it lets you stay in the same relative position while you lose excess altitude (just reduce power and continue circling) when, for example, you arrive at a destination far above pattern altitude. Contracted, of course, it lets you get close-up views of landmarks (as we are going to shortly) in as much detail as you want.

Don't give up. Take off from Manhattan Airport again, if necessary, and fly this mode until you know you can fly Turns Around a Point. They're really simple once you get the hang of it. Just remember, if you're flying ahead of the point, steepen your bank; if it's getting ahead of you, decrease the bank.

You can use the same banking technique to set up the turn initially, too. All you need to know is where the object you want to circle is in relation to your low wing. If you're ahead of it, enter and hold a steeper bank until it comes into view, and then stop it where you want it simply by decreasing the bank. If you're behind it, shallow your bank or fly level until you catch up with it, then bank toward it, and set up the turn.

Meanwhile, don't forget to watch your altitude. In the present scenario, that's 1000 feet. Remember: Throttle is your altitude control.

As you circled, you may have noticed a big airport upriver from the Manhattan Bridge (that river, by the way, is the East River). The airport is La Guardia, at the north end of the Borough of Queens.

At some point, whenever you're ready, roll out of your turn so the Trade Center towers are on the extreme right of your windshield. (Don't forget to return to a front view. Those turns and points can make you forget what is happening.) You will probably see the Statue of Liberty on the opposite edge of your view; if not, continue banking left until it appears there.

At this point the statue is just an upright block in the Hudson River. After the towers disappear off to your right, orient the plane so the Statue of Liberty is right in the center of your windshield.

As you fly, take a left rear or rear view of the World Trade Center towers and a right rear or direct rear view of the Manhattan Bridge. Views like this are nice, and they give you a feeling for where you are and where you're going in relation to the whole landscape.

Very soon, the simulator accesses the disk to pick up some detail, and the Statue of Liberty becomes three-dimensional—hewn right out of the block. As you know by now, our objective is to do Turns Around a Point, the point in this case being the renowned statue.

I suggest you get into position to circle the Statue of Liberty clockwise, just for the practice of point-turning to the right. Either way, you'll see it from every side.

But if you get too close, your bank will wipe out the view. Here are a few tips for getting in the optimum viewing configuration (press the Pause key while you read):

Maintain your 1000-foot altitude. As the statue comes closer, keep it about halfway between the center and right edge of your windshield. When it becomes three-dimensional and begins to disappear to your right, set up a right side view (assuming you're going to circle clockwise) immediately. As soon as the statue is visible, add a notch of up elevator and set up a 20- or 25-degree right bank. Then adjust as described earlier to get and keep your desired view, which will probably be ahead of or behind the wing—otherwise, the figure may be hidden.

Once you are fairly stable in your turn, take a radar view, and watch yourself go around.

Keeping the Statue of Liberty where you want her requires constant work and attention to the controls. You may need, by turns, extra-shallow and extra-steep banks. Also, don't be afraid to use power—in combination with lower elevator settings—to gain on the statue when a steep bank won't do the job. Congratulate yourself if you get a nice, stable, steady turn around this point, keeping roughly the same distance from the statue in all directions with relatively little adjustment of your controls.

When you are satisfied with what you have done, straighten up, and set a course to the left of the World Trade Center towers. Then when the Empire State Building comes into view, fly between the two landmarks. You will see La Guardia Airport straight ahead. And you will pass dramatically close to the towers along the way. Take a good look at them.

La Guardia has a runway whose numbers match those of Manhattan Airport, 4/22, so plan for a landing on Runway 22. Be sure to take left front and side views of the Empire State Building, and Central Park just beyond it, as you cross Manhattan.

When you're over the East River, turn left to a heading of 40 degrees and you'll be downwind in a right-hand pattern for 22. Your final approach will be over the section of the river called Flushing Bay.

Rock and a Hard Place

Cape Cod, MA (Local)

North: 17792. East: 22159. Altitude: 69. Pitch: 0. Bank: 0. Heading: Cessna 8. Heading: Piper 355. Airspeed: 0. Throttle: 0. Rudder: 32767. Ailerons: 32767. Flaps: 0. Elevators: 32767. Time: 15:00. Season: 2. Clouds: 0. Surface Wind: 17 kn., 60 deg.

Windy, isn't it?

Even though we're flying flight simulators, I nonetheless look askance at crashing. Yet I do crash once in a while—in part because I have to explore the limits of these machines and of the simulator geography in order to pass reliable information on to you. (Isn't that a beautiful excuse?)

In truth, I sometimes crash due to good old pilot error. I'm only human. But, having done an analysis of my crashes, I conclude that most have been the result of striving for perfection, which usually happens in one specific configuration: on final approach for a landing. My foremost pilot error is over-controlling in an attempt to cross the runway threshold perfectly lined up. I hate to land on the grass with a runway right there staring at me two or three feet away. The solution, of course, is to give priority to the quality of the landing rather than the precise lie of the runway.

But, as I've said before, landing the simulated Cessna or Piper is harder than landing the real thing, due mostly to the limitations of simulator perspective and to the inevitable lag in control response.

Takeoffs, on the other hand, rarely offer any problems and are about the same as prototype takeoffs—except for the one you're about to make.

Imagine that you were flying in this general area a couple of hours ago when sudden bad weather forced you to the ground. You made an emergency landing here on Race Point, at the tip of Cape Cod. The landing was fine—no damage. But now the weather has cleared, and you must get this airplane out of here. You are surrounded by sand dunes and patches of wild vegetation, and there is only one clear path for takeoff: straight ahead. (In Cessna, it looks just like a runway, and in Piper you will wish the clearing were moved a little further to the right.)

Your normal takeoff procedure will not work here. Take my advice: Don't try it. Imagine that you are not in a simulator but in a real aircraft. The emergency is real; if you crash into the water, you may die. And you will surely damage your airplane.

Here is what to do now: Prepare for the takeoff with your normal takeoff trim (two quick notches of up elevator), but put on two notches of flaps instead of one (that is 20 degrees in Cessna, 25 in Piper). Apply full power and then at 60 KIAS, instead of 80, rotate with two quick notches of elevator instead of one.

Wait a bit longer than usual to remove the back pressure you used for takeoff, and when you do, remember that you used two quick notches instead of one. Then dump your flaps a notch at a time. From there on everything is normal. Trim two additional notches down in Cessna, one in Piper, and you will be at operational neutral. Then reduce your power to 2105 in Cessna, and 2205 in Piper, and you should find yourself climbing at about 500 FPM.

Climb to 1500, then reduce power to fly straight and level. Reverse your direction, and head back toward Race Point. (In the real world there is an airport near Race Point, which you can find on maps or on the FAA sectional. But it isn't in the simulation, so we won't worry about it.)

We are going to follow the near shore of fishhook-shaped Cape Cod right around Cape Cod Bay to the mainland of Massachusetts. Use radar to line up with the shoreline, and try to fly far enough out so you can see Cape Cod out the left side as well as the front.

There really are lots of sand dunes down there, along with salt marshes, ponds, wild vegetation, patches of woods, and trails. And altogether there are five lighthouses just on the strip you are following.

The hooked shape of Cape Cod was created by glaciers that slid down from the north thousands of years ago. They carried with them boulders, stones, and other geologic debris, which were released when the glacier melted, forming this peninsula, which was then modified by centuries of wind and wave action.

Cape Cod used to be a haven for fishermen, whalers, and salt producers, and was the site of Guglielmo Marconi's first U.S. wireless station. On the Atlantic side is the main portion of the Cape Cod National Seashore, created by the U.S. government in 1961 to preserve the natural beauty of the area. There you can look on the limitless and timeless caprices of wave and weather.

Before you turn right to track the coastline, you will see two islands beyond Cape Cod. The one straight ahead is Nantucket, and to the right of that is Martha's Vineyard. The water is Nantucket Sound.

Now I'm going to show you how to use your two NAV systems to pinpoint a location, for a secret purpose I won't reveal just yet.

Press the Pause key

Tune NAV1 to Whitman VOR, 114.5, and center its OBI needle with a TO indication (making no turns yet, however).

Tune NAV2 to Martha's Vineyard VOR, 108.2, and center its OBI needle with a FROM indication. (You could use a TO radial here, but FROM fits the concept a bit better, and you will be flying away from the station at all times.)

When both OBI needles are centered, press the Pause key, and do the following:

Spread out your New York/Boston chart.

Using a pencil and a straightedge, draw a line intersecting the Whitman TO radial you are on, the center of the Whitman compass rose, and the resultant point on the Cape Cod shore. The line will, of course, split the Whitman compass rose in half.

Now draw another line, this time intersecting the Martha's Vineyard VOR, the FROM radial you are on, and the first line you drew.

Wherever in Cape Cod Bay or on the Cape Cod peninsula the lines intersect is precisely where you are at this moment. Press the Pause key, and take a look at radar to confirm the accuracy of your plot.

That's how, using two NAV systems and any two VOR stations within range, you can always determine your precise location on a sectional chart. So you see that the two NAVs are good for more than just backup.

Now, using the techniques you learned in an earlier chapter, do what you have to do to get on the 314 radial to Whitman, with the OBI needle centered. Go ahead and do that, and then come back.

Next, begin to include the NAV2 readings in your regular instrument scan and use the OBS to keep the OBI2 needle centered. (Be sure you are changing the NAV2 OBS, not the NAV1.)

Observe that because you are flying FROM Martha's Vineyard, the needle responds opposite to the usual direction. When it moves to the right, you are cranking the OBS left to center the needle again.

The Martha's Vineyard radial numbers decrease steadily as you correct, and your DME, which is indicating nautical miles from the Whitman OMNI, reads ever lower, naturally. There is no DME readout for NAV2.

Our ultimate destination is about 20 nautical miles from Whitman. Before too long, you will see the Boston metropolitan area on the right of your screen. But we are not going to Boston. You will also be able to spot Massachusetts State Highway 3, which roughly parallels the coastline.

You have a number of important jobs to keep up with: holding your altitude at 1500, keeping the OBI1 needle centered on the Whitman 314 radial, and regularly adjusting the Martha's Vineyard OBS to see what radial you're on. As you cross the 16 radial from the Martha's Vineyard VOR, immediately get into slowflight and prepare for a landing.

I realize there's no airport here, but trust me, and continue to follow my instructions.

Press the Pause key to get this straight: Our objective is to land as close as possible to the point at which the 314 radial from Whitman and the 10 radial from Martha's Vineyard intersect. This has nothing to do with the earlier lines you drew, but you can draw lines now to pinpoint the spot if you want to, though it won't help you land there. The elevation at the spot, which is marked only by our feverish staring, is about 590 feet. Make a full-flaps approach, and apply your brakes gently as soon as you're down. Press the Pause key now and shoot the landing.

How did you do?

If the upper OBI needle is centered on the 314 bearing and the Whitman OBI is centered on the 10 radial, you are amazing! And if you are off just a degree or two on either or both, you still did a fine job.

You can see that not only can two NAVs tell you exactly where you are, but flying them can put you exactly where you want to be, which in this case is the intersection of Whitman 314 and Martha's Vineyard 10.

So why did we land at this particular spot? Can you guess? Look out all sides. See anything?

Here are three clues: We took off from a hard place; this is a favored landing spot; and it has something, however remote, to do with Lee Iacocca.

One More Time

Forget parameters!

I'm determined to do one more thing before this book is finished. I want to make one last, very special excursion into the Bermuda triangle world of Eagle Field. My concept is this:

In "An Eerie Eyrie of Eagles" we took off from the World War I friendly airbase, on Runway 27, and flew absolutely straight, up over the mountain with the arrow on it, and, flying straight as an arrow, arrived at a clone of the Red Quiver Valley. A clone, in fact, of the exact area from which we took off, except that the clone was missing the runway and hangar.

At that time I recorded—not just for myself but for history—the parameters of my Eagle Field Clone 1 position.

If you remember, when I came to a stop in the vicinity of where the runway was supposed to be but wasn't, my North position was 17421 and my East position was 7193. And that was quite a distance from the original Eagle Field.

My idea now is to use the Editor to position ourselves, not at Eagle Field, but at Eagle Field Clone 1. And having done that, we'll reverse direction and fly back to the original Eagle Field, retracing our earlier flight but on the opposite heading.

You see, if we took off straight ahead—from the clone, that is—we wouldn't get back to Eagle Field; we would just come to another clone. But in the opposite direction, the North and East parameters will wind down to put us on approach—not to Runway 27, I guess, but to the reciprocal, Runway 9. This will mean a tough approach, because we will need considerable altitude to clear the mountain, and will then have to let down in a hurry. But, on the other hand, we can circle over Red Quiver Valley to lose altitude, so everything should be fine.

I assume that we'll approach Eagle Field (the original) from the west, because our heading will be east from Clone 1. But anything can happen here in the Eagle Field Triangle, or octagonal, or whatever kind of polygon it is. So, be prepared for anything. Among other things, we will discover whether Clone 1 has a hangar and runway when entered afresh from the Editor.

Follow this procedure so we'll all be in the same groove:

1. Go into the Editor.

2. At User Mode, enter a 0, unless the 0 mode is already in effect. This will return everything to the power-up status.

3. Skip down to North and enter the parameter I recorded after my landing at Clone 1—17421.

Press the Editor key

4. Enter the East parameter likewise — 7193.

5. Set altitude to 410.

6. Set heading to 90.

7. Save the parameters you've entered.

Leave everything else just as it is, and exit the Editor.

Make sure you're heading 90 degrees. If your carb heat is still on from the previous chapter, correct it (carb heat doesn't turn off when you're in the Editor, which is why you should always check it prior to takeoff).

Take a good look around you. Everything — the gridlines and the mountains behind you — seems to be where it's supposed to be. We have simply done an about-face. But, just as we might have expected, the runway and hangar are still missing.

Let's waste no time. We are headed for our rendezvous with Eagle Field. Ready your plane, and take off straight ahead.

But don't trim down at all after you rotate. Keep your takeoff trim and full power, just as we did when we departed Eagle on the original flight. We don't have a mountain to clear this time, but we want 6500 feet of altitude as soon as possible, because we may have a mountain to clear at the other end of our trip.

Do, however, dump your flaps as soon as you're climbing 500 FPM, and look back at Clonesville as you ascend. Get straight and level at 6500.

This time, instead of gazing backward until the area disappears, we'll keep watching forward and see it appear — or reappear.

It just seemed to grow out of the landscape, didn't it? As if at some sort of signal. Now to find out if the runway and hangar are still there.

It seems as if the best way to do this would be to start our let down now and forget crossing the peak; just aim over to your left where the ridge reaches its lowest point, and we'll cross the mountain there.

Even after we're on the other side of the mountain, it's still hard to tell if this is the real Eagle Field. We can't see a runway or hangar yet, but we are still a number of miles away. Head for the approximate location of the runway as you remember it, and continue your descent.

The miles tick away. But where is Eagle?

Ah, there it is. Sprawled, like a smashed spider.

There is no wind, so plan to land on Runway 9. And once you're down, come back here for a minute.

Press the Editor key

Press the Recall key

I don't think the exploration of Red Quiver Valley and Eagle Field and the other airports here will ever be really complete. But I know for sure that this exercise we have just finished is really not finished.

This flight didn't last too long, and we are already (almost) set up in the Editor. So, if you're with me, let's make one final reconnaissance:

Let's fly 270 degrees—not from here, but from Clone 1, that is, let's fly a second leg in the original direction and see if any airport shows up. If that gets us back to Eagle Field, we'll have learned something. And if it doesn't, we will have learned something else. Are you with me?

OK. So enter the Editor, press Recall, which re-establishes our location at hangarless, runwayless Clone 1, and change only heading, to 270. Then exit the Editor.

Take off again, over the mountain, keeping all your takeoff trim as before. Just dump your flaps as you climb, and hang in there.

Once you have cleared the mountain, fly at the altitude you want. You know how to fly the airplane now. You know how to hustle around the sky, control your airspeed and altitude like a pro, use your eyes and your mind and the skills you have developed. You know how to fly.

Yes, and sure enough, there is another valley ahead of us—another backdrop of mountains, no matter how make believe, and, perhaps, another runway. But always, a pinch in the heart, a twinge of high anticipation, an exultation in the new, the unknown, the sometimes unknowable. What mystery, what beauty, what challenge lies ahead in this next microcosm of the world?

· And how beautiful this simulator world is, that can take us in imagination to faraway places where in reality we would never be able to go. There are rivers and lakes and hills and stretches of beach out there that we haven't seen. And cities we believe in, no matter how drab, featureless, and unsupportive of life they seem to be. And earth and sky that stretch to everywhere—beyond our ability to witness the limit of them, inviting us to accept them for exactly what they are: luxuriantly green, endlessly blue, beckoning us to survive so we may yet discover. And all of it is ours just for the asking.

Thanks for the pleasure of flying with you.

AIRCRAFT
CONTROLS

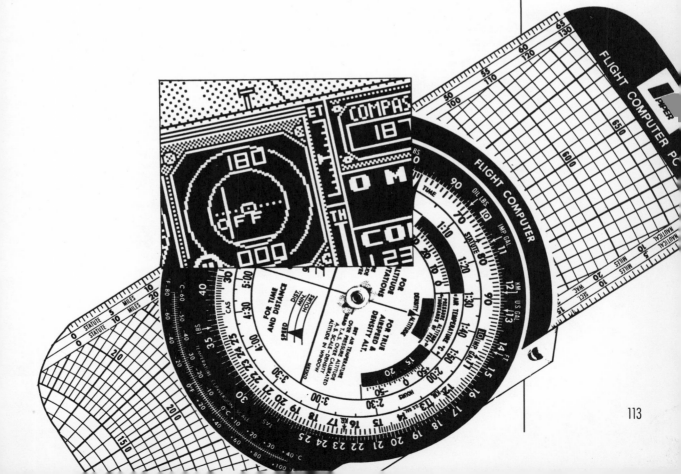

Apple Aircraft Controls

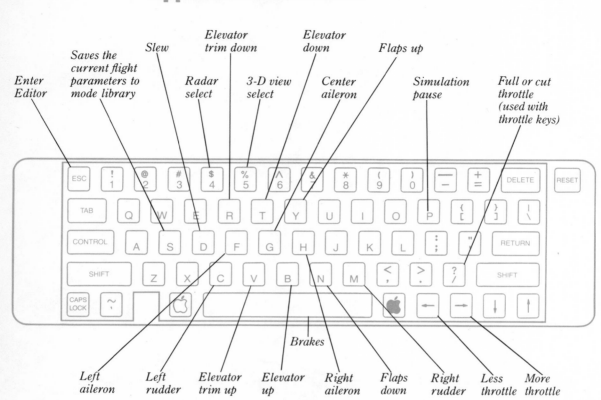

Enter
Editor

Saves the
current flight
parameters to
mode library

Slew

Radar
select

Elevator
trim down

3-D view
select

Elevator
down

Center
aileron

Flaps up

Simulation
pause

Full or cut
throttle
(used with
throttle keys)

Brakes

Left
aileron

Left
rudder

Elevator
trim up

Elevator
up

Right
aileron

Flaps
down

Right
rudder

Less
throttle

More
throttle

For additional controls, press CTRL or SHIFT and one or more keys:

Keys	Result
CTRL B	Adjusts the altimeter
CTRL D	Adjusts the heading indicator
CTRL L	Toggles the lights on or off
CTRL X	Recalls mode library from disk
CTRL Z	Saves mode library to disk
SHIFT +	Recalls mode from library (resets the simulator)

View Selector Controls for the Apple

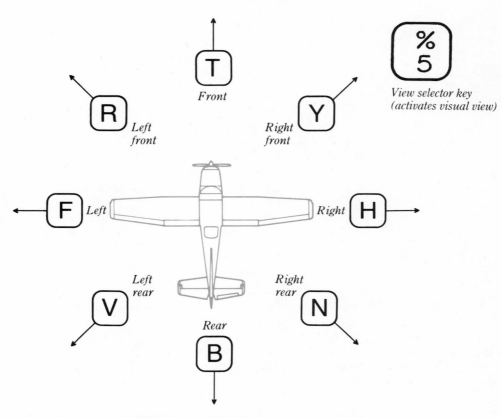

For radio controls, press CTRL and one or more keys:

COM radio	CTRL C, >>>	Increase high digits (<<< for decrease)
	CTRL C, CRTL C, >>>	Increase low digits
NAV radio	CTRL N, 1	Select NAV1 for frequency changes
	CTRL N, 2	Select NAV2
	CTRL N, >>>	Increase high digits on selected NAV radio (<<< for decrease)
	CTRL N, CTRL N, >>>	Increase low digits
ADF	CTRL A, >>>	Rapidly press one, two, or three times to select digits 1, 2, or 3
VORS OBS	CTRL V, 1	Select VOR OBS1
	CTRL V, 2	Select VOR OBS2
	CTRL V, >>>	Increase bearing (<<< for decrease)
Transponder	CTRL T	Rapidly press one, two, three, or four times to select digits 1, 2, 3, or 4
	CTRL T, >>>	Increase digit (<<< for decrease)

Note: CTRL X is treated as CTRL T

Atari Aircraft Controls

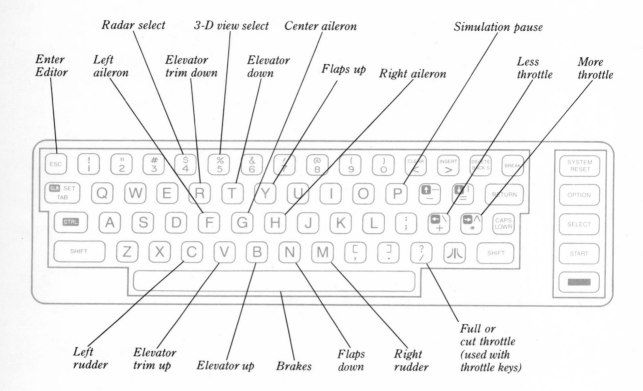

Radar select 3-D view select Center aileron Simulation pause

Enter Editor Left aileron Elevator trim down Elevator down Flaps up Right aileron Less throttle More throttle

Left rudder Elevator trim up Elevator up Brakes Flaps down Right rudder Full or cut throttle (used with throttle keys)

For radio controls, press CTRL and one or more keys:

COM radio	CTRL C, >>>	Increase high digits (<<< for decrease)
	CTRL C, CRTL C, >>>	Increase low digits
NAV radio	CTRL N, 1	Select NAV1 for frequency changes
	CTRL N, 2	Select NAV2
	CTRL N, >>>	Increase high digits on selected NAV radio (<<< for decrease)
	CTRL N, CTRL N, >>>	Increase low digits
ADF	CTRL A, >>>	Rapidly press one, two, or three times to select digits 1, 2, or 3
VORS OBS	CTRL V, 1	Select VOR OBS1
	CTRL V, 2	Select VOR OBS2
	CTRL V, >>>	Increase bearing (<<< for decrease)
Transponder	CTRL T	Rapidly press one, two, three, or four times to select digits 1, 2, 3, or 4
	CTRL T, >>>	Increase digit (<<< for decrease)

Note: CTRL X is treated as CTRL T.

View Selector Controls for the Atari

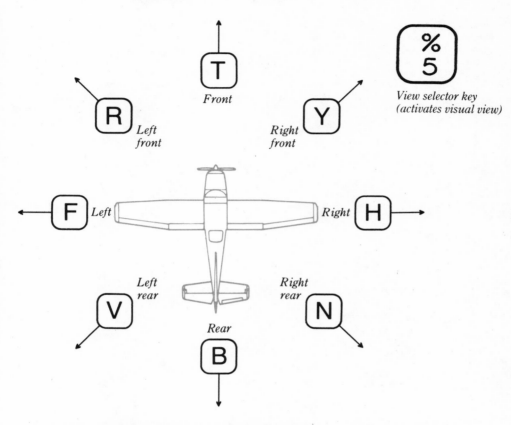

Front

Left front

Right front

%
5

*View selector key
(activates visual view)*

Left

Right

Left rear

Right rear

Rear

For additional controls, press CTRL and one or more keys:

Keys	Result
CTRL B	Adjusts the altimeter
CTRL D	Adjusts the heading indicator
CTRL E	Logs in the Scenery Disk
CTRL L	Toggles the lights on or off
CTRL S	Saves the current flight parameters to mode library
CTRL X	Recalls mode library from disk
CTRL Z	Saves mode library to disk
CTRL =	Recalls mode from library (resets the simulator)

Commodore 64 Aircraft Controls

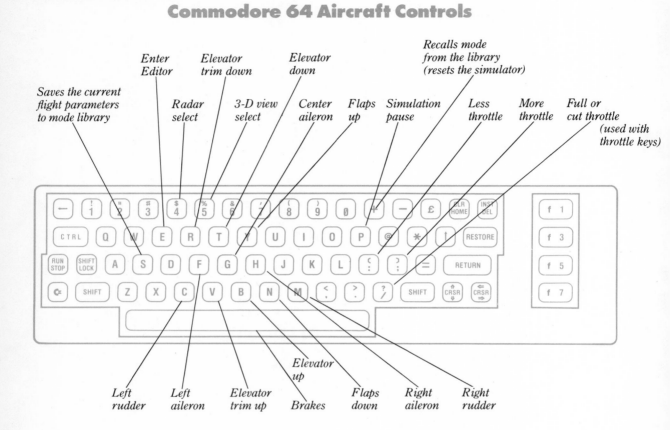

Enter Editor

Elevator trim down

Elevator down

Recalls mode from the library (resets the simulator)

Saves the current flight parameters to mode library

Radar select

3-D view select

Center aileron

Flaps up

Simulation pause

Less throttle

More throttle

Full or cut throttle (used with throttle keys)

Left rudder

Left aileron

Elevator trim up

Elevator up

Brakes

Flaps down

Right aileron

Right rudder

For additional controls, press CTRL and one or more keys:

Keys	Result
CTRL B	Adjusts the altimeter
CTRL D	Adjusts the heading indicator
CTRL E	Logs in the Scenery Disk
CTRL L	Toggles the lights on or off
CTRL S	Saves the current flight parameters to mode library
CTRL X	Recalls mode library from disk
CTRL Z	Saves mode library to disk

Note: CTRL X and CTRL Z only work while you are in the Editor

View Selector Controls for the Commodore 64

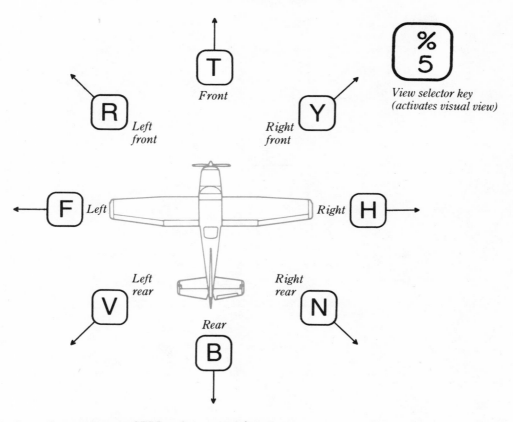

For radio controls, press CTRL and one or more keys:

COM radio	CTRL C, >>>	Increase high digits (<<< for decrease)
	CTRL C, CRTL C, >>>	Increase low digits
NAV radio	CTRL N, 1	Select NAV1 for frequency changes
	CTRL N, 2	Select NAV2
	CTRL N, >>>	Increase high digits on selected NAV radio (<<< for decrease)
	CTRL N, CTRL N, >>>	Increase low digits
ADF	CTRL A, >>>	Rapidly press one, two, or three times to select digits 1, 2, or 3
VORS OBS	CTRL V, 1	Select VOR OBS1
	CTRL V, 2	Select VOR OBS2
	CTRL V, >>>	Increase bearing (<<< for decrease)
Transponder	CTRL T	Rapidly press one, two, three, or four times to select digits 1, 2, 3, or 4
	CTRL T, >>>	Increase digit (<<< for decrease)

Note: CTRL X is treated as CTRL T

IBM PC Aircraft Controls

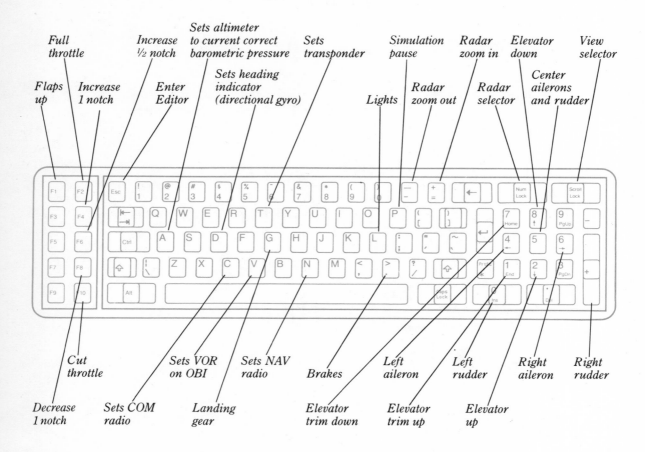

For the following controls enter the Editor and press one of these keys:

Key	Result
Ins	Saves the current flight parameters to mode library
S	Saves the mode library to disk
PrtSc	Loads the flight parameters from mode library
L	Recalls mode library from disk

View Selector Controls for the IBM PC

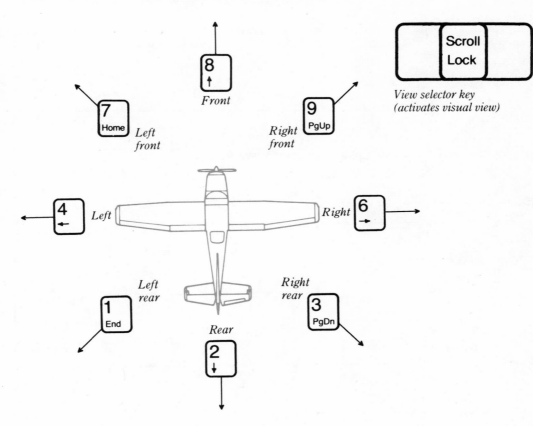

Front

Left front

Right front

Left

Right

Left rear

Right rear

Rear

Scroll Lock

View selector key (activates visual view)

IBM PCjr Aircraft Controls

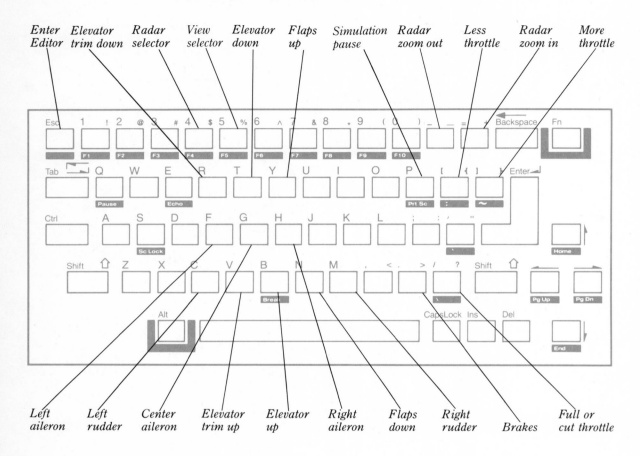

Enter Editor · Elevator trim down · Radar selector · View selector · Elevator down · Flaps up · Simulation pause · Radar zoom out · Less throttle · Radar zoom in · More throttle

Left aileron · Left rudder · Center aileron · Elevator trim up · Elevator up · Right aileron · Flaps down · Right rudder · Brakes · Full or cut throttle

For additional controls, press SHIFT and one of these keys:

Keys	Result
SHIFT A	Sets the altimeter to the current barometric pressure
SHIFT C	Sets the COM radio frequency
SHIFT D	Sets the heading indicator (directional gyro) to the magnetic compass
SHIFT G	Raises or lowers the landing gear
SHIFT L	Toggles the instrument and running lights on or off
SHIFT N	Sets the NAV radio frequency
SHIFT T	Sets the transponder "squawk"
SHIFT V	Sets the OBI to a VOR frequency

View Selector Controls for the IBM PCjr

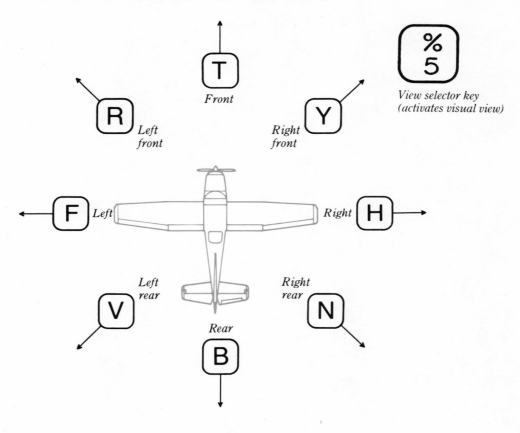

View selector key (activates visual view)

For the following controls enter the Editor and press one of these keys:

Key	Result
Ins	Saves the current flight parameters to mode library
S	Saves the mode library to disk
PrtSc	Loads the flight parameters from mode library
L	Recalls mode library from disk

Glossary

Active runway: (Often shortened to simply "the active.") The runway in use, based primarily on wind conditions and occasionally on traffic conditions. When more than one runway is in use, smaller aircraft are typically required to use the shortest runway.

AGL: Above Ground Level. Used to describe an aircraft's altitude above the ground. Aircraft instruments do not provide the pilot with this information. Altitude AGL must be deduced from a reading of the altimeter and charts or knowledge of the terrain over which the aircraft is operating.

Ailerons: Pilot-controllable surfaces on the rear or trailing edge of each wing, used to roll the aircraft and thus turn it. Acting in opposite directions, they increase lift on one wing while decreasing it on the other, causing the aircraft to roll on its longitudinal axis, then bank and turn in the direction of the lower wing.

Airfoil: A structural shape which creates or contributes to lift, such as the shape of an aircraft's wings and tail surfaces.

Airspeed indicator: A panel instrument notifying the pilot of the aircraft's rate of speed through the air. It operates by measuring the pressure of the relative wind against the wings. Indicated airspeed is not true airspeed nor is it the same as ground speed.

Altimeter: A panel instrument which tells the pilot the aircraft's altitude above sea level, also referred to as MSL (Mean Sea Level) altitude. The altimeter operates by measuring decreases or increases in atmospheric pressure, respectively, as the aircraft climbs or descends.

Angle of attack: The angle between the relative wind and the chord line of a wing or other airfoil. The chord line is an imaginary line through the center of an airfoil, drawn from the leading to the trailing edge.

Artificial horizon: A panel instrument depicting an aircraft's attitude with respect to the earth's horizon. It continuously updates and displays a symbol of the horizon, and of the aircraft's wings and nose in relation to that horizon.

ATC: Air Traffic Control. A ground-based radio network at many (but not all) airports, consisting of: Ground Control, which provides taxiing instructions; Tower, which provides instructions and clearances (permission) for takeoffs and landings; Departure Control and Approach Control, for the airspace immediately surrounding the airport; and Center, which controls the airspace at higher altitudes. Flight Simulator procedures cover only the Tower portion of the network, and that only to a minor degree.

ATIS: Automatic Terminal Information Service. A radio aid providing weather and other information about a given airport, including the designation of the active runway.

Atmospheric pressure: The pressure exerted on the earth by its atmosphere. Also termed "barometric pressure" because it is measured by a barometric device.

Auto-coordination: A system by which the ailerons and rudder of an aircraft are interconnected, so that control of one automatically provides coordinated control of the other, eliminating skidding or slipping in turns.

Bank: The lateral tilting of an aircraft—the result of rolling it about its longitudinal axis—which causes it to turn in the direction of the lower wing. The roll is begun by application of aileron in the desired direction of bank and turn.

Bleed off: To decrease a value, such as airspeed or altitude, in a slow and controlled manner.

Ceiling: The altitude at which the bottom boundary of the lowest cloud layer in an overcast will be encountered.

COM: Short for Communications. In Flight Simulator, the communications radio.

Control yoke: See Yoke.

Crabbing: A condition of flight in which, due to the direction of the winds aloft, the aircraft is moving somewhat sideways through the air, but following a straight line in relation to the ground. Named after the manner in which crabs move.

Density altitude: Pressure altitude (as shown on an altimeter) referenced to temperature, for computing aircraft performance.

Directional gyro: See Heading indicator.

DME: Distance Measuring Equipment, providing the pilot with a panel readout of the aircraft's distance from a VOR station, in nautical miles.

Drag: Forces that oppose an aircraft's movement through the air, acting parallel to, and in the same direction as, the relative wind.

Elevators: Pilot-controllable surfaces on the trailing edge of the horizontal stabilizer, used to pitch the aircraft's nose up or down, or keep it level with the horizon, thus controlling airspeed. The elevators are controlled by the yoke. Pulling back on the yoke moves the elevators up, and the relative wind forces the tail downward while the nose pitches up. Releasing back pressure or applying forward pressure on the yoke produces the opposite result.

FAA: Federal Aviation Administration.

Flaps: Pilot-controllable airfoils on the trailing edge of the wings, used to assist the pilot in takeoffs, slowflight, and landings. On takeoff, lowering or extending the flaps by 10 degrees (nominal) provides the highest lift-to-drag ratio, shortening the distance required to get airborne. Lowered flaps assist in slowflight by increasing drag and at the same time reducing the aircraft's stalling speed. On landing approaches, flaps are lowered—typically all the way—to accommodate a steeper angle of descent, for instance for clearing obstacles or flying tight airport patterns. Flaps also permit touchdown at a lower airspeed, because of a higher coefficient of lift and thus a lower stalling airspeed. After touchdown, the drag of the flaps shortens the landing roll.

Flare: The leveling-off phase of a landing approach, just prior to touchdown, bringing the aircraft level or slightly nose-high. It is performed a foot or so above the runway in actual aircraft, but somewhat higher than that in the simulator to compensate for the relative insensitivity and slow reaction-time of the simulated control.

FPM: Feet Per Minute. Used to measure an aircraft's rate of climb or descent.

Gear: See Landing gear.

Glideslope: A navigation aid used on ILS landing approaches, consisting of a horizontal needle which displays the correct vertical position for the aircraft in its approach to the runway threshold. The pilot works to keep the needle centered by continuously monitoring his angle of descent, and adjusting it as required. The glideslope is used in conjunction with the localizer.

Ground speed: An aircraft's actual speed over the ground, which is not available as an instrument readout but must be calculated.

Heading: The magnetic compass direction in which the aircraft is pointed, in relation to a 360-degree circle. It is not necessarily the direction the aircraft is traveling (see, for instance, Crabbing).

Heading indicator: (Also called the directional gyro.) A compass controlled by a gyroscope, which gives the pilot heading information based on forces which act on the gyro rather than on magnetic readings. It obviates the lag inherent in a magnetic compass, and requires no settling time, as does the latter, after turns and climbs.

Horizontal stabilizer: The fixed horizontal surface at the rear of the aircraft, equipped with controllable elevators.

IAS: Indicated Air Speed. Also see KIAS.

IFR: Instrument Flight Rules. The rules by which an aircraft must be flown when in instrument conditions, or when flight by visual reference (see VFR) is difficult or impossible.

ILS: Instrument Landing System. A system of radio aids that displays, on the pilot's instrument panel, three-dimensional references by which he can make an approach and landing without outside visual references. It consists of a localizer, glideslope, marker beacons, and approach lights (the latter not included in the Flight Simulators).

KIAS: Knots Indicated Air Speed. An aircraft's airspeed in knots per hour, as read on the airspeed indicator.

Knots: Nautical miles per hour, abbreviated kn. A knot is equal to 1.1507 statute miles, or conversely, a statute mile is equal to .869 knots. The simulator airspeed indicator and the DME read in knots.

Landing gear: The appendage of struts and wheels on which the airplane lands. Both the simulated Cessna and Piper aircraft have "tricycle" gear, comprised of a nose wheel and two main wheels, which enable the aircraft to sit level on the ground. Landings should, however, be made on the main wheels, with the nose wheel being lowered to the runway only after the plane has landed and slowed down.

Localizer: A radio navigational aid used in conjunction with the glideslope on ILS landing approaches. The localizer needle is a vertical needle which displays the correct horizontal position for the aircraft on its approach to the runway threshold. The pilot works to keep the needle centered, by continuously monitoring his heading and adjusting it as required.

Magneto: A device that creates the high voltages required for aircraft engine spark plugs. It combines the functions of an automobile engine's coil and distributor.

Marker beacons: Labeled O, M, and I on the instrument panel, Outer, Middle, and Inner marker beacons consist of visible and audible signals which tell the pilot his relative distance from the end of the runway on ILS approaches.

NAV: Short for Navigation. In Flight Simulator, the navigation radios (NAV1 and NAV2).

OBI: Omni-Bearing Indicator. A panel instrument that gives the pilot information about the aircraft's position relative to the VOR station to which the NAV radio is tuned. It consists of an OBS or Omni-Bearing Selector for selecting a course or radial; a to-from indicator, advising whether the pilot is flying toward or away from the station; a CDI or Course Deviation Indicator (or "needle" for short) which the pilot works to keep centered; and in the case of NAV1, glideslope and localizer (glidepath) needles which indicate, respectively, the correct vertical and horizontal courses to the runway threshold on an ILS approach.

OMNI: Short for Omni-Bearing Indicator and/or its components, and also, loosely, a VOR station.

Phonetic alphabet: The terms used to transmit letters and numbers via aircraft radio, to prevent misundertandings:

A	Alpha	N	November	1	Wun
B	Bravo	O	Oscar	2	Too
C	Charlie	P	Papa	3	Tree
D	Delta	Q	Quebec	4	Fower
E	Echo	R	Romeo	5	Five
F	Foxtrot	S	Sierra	6	Six
G	Golf	T	Tango	7	Seven
H	Hotel	U	Uniform	8	Aight
I	India	V	Victor	9	Niner
J	Juliet	W	Whiskey	0	Zeeroh
K	Kilo	X	X-Ray		
L	Lima	Y	Yankee		
M	Mike	Z	Zulu		

Note that numbers are spoken as individual digits. For example, 297 is spoken "too niner seven."

Pitch: The angle between the longitudinal axis of the aircraft and the horizon. Pitch is described as "nose up," "nose down," and "level." We also say an aircraft is "pitched up" or "pitched down."

Power setting: The amount of throttle, or fuel flow, applied to the engine, determined in the prototype by the position of the throttle (a push-pull control), and in the simulator by the number of notches applied to the throttle.

Rate of climb: The rate at which the airplane is climbing, measured in feet per minute. Also used, illogically, to define the rate at which the airplane is descending, though "rate of descent" is better applied to that condition. There can, however, be a zero rate of climb without confusion.

Rate of climb indicator: See VSI.

Rate of turn: The rate at which the aircraft is turning, measured in degrees per second, as a result of its airspeed and the sideways force, or horizontal lift component, which is causing it to turn. The rate of turn at any given airspeed is controlled by the angle of bank.

Rotation: The act of rotating the aircraft on takeoff, or using back pressure to raise the nose just prior to departing the ground. The aircraft is rotated as it reaches climb speed.

RPM: Revolutions Per Minute. The measure of the speed at which the aircraft's engine, and the propeller fastened to its crankshaft, are turning, as a result of the amount of throttle applied, the aircraft's pitch, and other flight conditions.

Rudder: Pilot-controllable surface on the trailing edge of the vertical stabilizer that controls yaw, or rotation about the aircraft's vertical axis.

Skid: A sliding of the aircraft to the left or right, out of alignment with the desired flight path. A skidding turn results when centrifugal force is greater than horizontal lift, pulling the aircraft toward the outside of the turn.

Slip: A yawing of the aircraft toward the outside of the path of a turn. A slipping turn results when horizontal lift is greater than centrifugal force.

Stack: (Also called "radio stack.") The section of the instrument panel where the COM, NAV and transponder are installed, usually in a stack on top of one another.

Tachometer: Often abbreviated "tach." The instrument that measures the speed of rotation of the engine, in revolutions per minute (RPM).

TAS: True Air Speed. Airspeed after compensation for density altitude.

Taxi: To move an aircraft on the ground.

Throttle: The control that determines the speed of rotation of the engine's crankshaft, in revolutions per minute, by the rate at which it permits fuel to flow.

Trim: Small control surfaces affecting the elevators, making it unnecessary to maintain pressures on the yoke. In this book, trim is simulated by elevator settings, since no pressures can be felt in the simulator.

Vertical stabilizer: (Also called the "fin.") A fixed vertical surface at the rear of the aircraft, to which a movable surface—the rudder—is hinged. The vertical stabilizer helps to stabilize the aircraft in the vertical or yaw axis.

VFR: Visual Flight Rules. Rules covering flights in visual conditions, or conditions when visual references are adequate for safe control of an aircraft. Compare IFR.

VOR: Very high frequency Omnidirectional Range. A radio transmission system provided for pilots which enables them, with the necessary equipment, to navigate along or over magnetic course radials (all of which converge at specific VOR stations), and thus to navigate precisely throughout the airspace.

VOR station: The facility housing a VOR transmission system and equipment. Each VOR station has a name, usually that of an airport or nearby town.

VSI: Vertical Speed Indicator. A panel instrument showing the aircraft's rate of ascent or descent, in feet per minute.

Yaw: An aircraft's rotation about its vertical axis. The vertical axis is also called the yaw axis.

Yoke: The pilot's control column, similar in appearance (but not performance) to an automobile steering wheel. The yoke incorporates aileron and elevator control, resulting from "pressures" applied by the pilot. The term "pressure" stresses the fact that the yoke is not pushed, pulled or turned abruptly or forcefully, but moved slowly and in small increments. Pressures to left or right operate the ailerons. Backward or forward pressures operate the elevators. The yoke returns to its neutral position when pressure is released.

CHARLES GULICK

In addition to **THE FLIGHT SIMULATOR CO-PILOT**, Charles Gulick is the author of the popular *40 Great Flight Simulator Adventures* and *40 More Great Flight Simulator Adventures,* published by Compute! Books. He has also written software and hardware reviews, and a program, "Peek Pong," for *80 Micro* magazine. Charles Gulick lives in Lake Park, Florida.

The manuscript for this book was prepared and submitted to Microsoft Press in electronic form. Text files were processed and formatted using Microsoft Word.

Cover design by Becker Design Associates

Interior text design by Becker Design Associates

Principal typographer: Bonnie Dunham

Principal production artist: Gloria Sommer

Text composition by Microsoft Press in Century Old Style, using the CCI composition system and the Mergenthaler Linotron 202 digital phototypesetter.